Verney Junction
to
Baker Street

In Celebration of 150 years of
the
World's First Underground Railway

BILL SIMPSON

Published by
Lamplight Publications
260 Colwell Drive, Witney
Oxfordshire OX28 5LW

First published 2013

ISBN: 978 1 899246 57 1

Printed and bound at Berforts Information Press
Southfield Road, Eynsham, Oxford OX29 4JB

Contents

Acknowledgements

The Author would like to express his thanks to the following in support of his work on the publication of this book.

R K Blencowe, Robert Boyd, Andrew Bratton, R M Casserley, Railway Gazette, Francis Hanford (Curator, Royal Air Force Museum at Halton Camp). London Transport Society. R H G Meredith, Quainton Railway Society, G K Kerley, Rob Riley, In memory of the late Dudley Rudd. R H G Simpson, Laura Sleath (Curator London Transport Museum), Neil Sprinks, Barry Tucker.

Introduction

It is very fitting the London Transport Museum together with the Buckinghamshire Railway Centre are celebrating the opening of the London Underground 150 years ago. It is a system very much taken for granted and more often criticised when it fails because it works so well. If one could imagine being on a platform at the periphery of the city and descending vertically being able to see the vastness of this system in a kind of massive transparent amphitheatre it would be a staggering visual experience.

Railways, escalators, lifts and people all in continuous movement the interconnection of trains moving at high speed like pulses of light on intricate microcircuitry. A complexity that is repeated daily and is the bloodstream of the life of the city.

Charles Pearson who insisted that the solution to London's congestion problems was to go beneath the streets would look now and see the problem repeating itself. However, how would those streets now have been without this essential support network?

Not least in wartime, Pearson could never imagine that his concept would save the lives of thousands of Londoners during the bombing in World War Two.

As the city celebrates many state occasions so it becomes the Underground to adjust to the expanded demand, often not with comfort, but speed ensures that the discomfort is minimised. The staff of the Underground apply their years of experience to the tasks and enormous numbers of people are moved around with a minimum of fuss and in complete safety. It is a triumph that we as a nation seldom give recognition to, so it is so fitting that the limelight is for once shone on the railway beneath our feet.

Its expansion into greater London and beyond is now firmly fixed to the public imagination as the myth of 'Metroland'. A commercial venture that succeeded in spinning the perfect metaphor to rouse our primal longings for arboreal enclosure in secure homesteads. Not quite so individual as it was based on mass transit.

The contrast with the remote looking glass world north of Aylesbury could not be more marked. A place where hardened city gents could happily lose their reason to their eccentricities. Where cricket is played too long into fading summer light near slow turning windmills and the chimes of Evensong drifts across the patchwork of fields.

Quainton, Waddesdon, Botolph Claydon, Steeple Claydon, Upper Pollicot, Lower Pollicot, Brill, Wotton; and why does the muse always arise in the mind when one mentions Verney Junction? A station fittingly odd with just a few buildings surrounding it, though fine buildings they are, especially the village pub that deserves more patronage than it gets.

This was a place without urgency, where summer haze could hide the distance of straight parallel lines of railway. A place to linger and nourish the soul admiring the varied coloured blooms of a carefully tended station garden. Whilst the only sound apart from cattle and birdsong comes from the delicate tinkle of the signalbox block bell out of the darkness of its open window.

A sanguine liveried engine murmurs in steam with its cinnamon coloured coaches and eventually leaves, almost apologetically, with least disturbance.

An arrival from a country walk would surprise one a great deal to see on its side 'Metropolitan Railway' for the train would be destained for Baker Street or Aldgate. Bewilderingly, for it seems to be at odds with an area fifty miles from the City. By chance an early rather ramshackle local railway was taken over and became the dream of expanded suburbs that was never realised. It is a place largely un-trammelled by modernity as it seems to distill a perfect sense of rural England. For which the poet the late Sir John Betjeman expressed he was glad. And so should we.

Bill Simpson

The look of Verney Junction in late Metropolitan period although the image repeats occasions in earlier years. The Jones 4-4-4 waits to leave for Rickmansworth, with a train for the City. An ex-LNWR 2-4-2 tank arrives from Bletchley to travel to Oxford. The Staionmaster's house of Met&GCR Joint Committee is behind the Met train. Whilst to the right is the house that still remains, formerly of the Aylesbury & Buckinghamshire Railway.

H C Casserley

In Distant Fields

Verney Junction, Winslow Road, Grandboro Road

The Vale of Aylesbury north of Aylesbury seems always an area never too precisely defined which is part of its charm, it hinters to the Oxfordshire border in the west, wanders amongst the Claydons in the north and in the east encounters the delightful settlements of Winslow and Stewkley. It is an area only lightly investigated by the tourist trek as it does not have what in the modern sense would be termed the 'beaten path'. An area easily imagined as the setting of ideal Arcadian summers. This is of course a town dwellers illusion, for the countryside was just as hard driven by the working demands of long hours of agricultural labour but retaining all that we like to imagine and cherish of rural England. The spires and towers of churches stand as spiritual markers on the landscape of hedge enclosing fields, modest in architecture, but reassuring, as we would be at a loss without them.

The intrusion of the railway soon melded into this landscape and adjusted in a unique way. Unlike the motor car that in early days went coughing and spluttering by with its driver complaining about the condition of the roads, as the local workers raised their heads and wondered in dismay of such foolishness that disturbed the enduring silence. Apart from bird song this was the silence of country ease, impossible to imagine now in this more discordant age.

The arrival of the lonesome aviator was rarer still. If the locals noticed it at all in their field labours it would be to raise an ear and with puzzled shaded eyes scorn the wantonness of man to impose his machinations into the sanctity of God's heaven.

However, after 1868 the sounds of the exhaust of locomotives with coaches and clanking wagons became very much part of daily repetition. This slow march of time that passed through thirty or forty years had to meet a very different pace in the middle of the twentieth century.

When I first visited Verney Junction in 1975 it still had the double track on the Oxford to Bletchley line with two platforms, with no track at the face of the one that had been for

Metropolitan line trains. The house remains outstanding with its small separate ticket office building both of which have survived in private ownership. I little realised at the time but this is similar to how it looked when it was first opened in 1868. The parsimonious Aylesbury & Buckingham Railway being able to afford little more. Issue of tickets and shelter facilities for passengers existed only in the Stationmaster's house.

The railway had been insisted upon by Sir Harry Verney, who lived at Claydon House close by, as the unrealised connection between the towns of Buckingham on the branch to Banbury, and the county town of Aylesbury. But it was a tenuous connection that had struggled to attract sufficient capital which enabled it only to build the line itself with precious little in the way of facilities.

When the GWR arrived at Aylesbury in 1863 the A&BR managed to compound an agreement that they would run its three return trains each day when it opened in 1868.

The LNWR that operated the line between Oxford and Bletchley resented this connection from the outset as they wanted all Aylesbury traffic to go circuitously via Cheddington on their main line. They would have been even less happy to have the GWR probing into what they considered to be their territory. The antagonising between early railway companies on territory was nothing short of tribal!

However as will be described later, the little company was to find salvation from another quarter that could not be so easily resisted.

The three stations between Aylesbury and Verney junction would have fared little better than the junction station. Small crossing keeper's houses were built as each was situated with a road crossing, a road being essential for trade access, milk collection being an expanding potential. The work of the keeper would be to issue tickets and deal with trade for the railway company as well.

Each station name was suffixed with the name 'Road' hinting at their remoteness.

The first called Winslow Road would be hard pressed to compete with the Winslow station of the LNWR on the aforementioned Oxford line.

Grandborough Road in terms of passenger numbers and must have served largely for farm trade only.

Quainton Road became the most significant station as will be described in the next chapter.

The final station to be built was at the behest of the Rothschild family that built Waddesdon Manor in 1889. A new station was built essentially for the convenience of the house and opened on January 1, 1897. By which time the line had been doubled by the Metropolitan Railway that took over running the line and relaid it with better rail.

The line to Aylesbury and Verney Junction was owned by the Met but leased to the Met & GCR Joint Committee. After World War 1 there was something of a mood to restore the golden age of before the war and in 1920 they continued to operate services between Aldgate and Verney Junction including the Pullman service. Electric to Rickmansworth, changing to a Jones 4-4-4 tank engine for the rest of the journey. The post war service did not include the Pullman service as far as Verney Junction.

However, the gold become an orange twilight as the passenger service between Quainton and Verney Junction ran for the last time on July 4, 1936 closing all stations beyond Quainton Road.

(324)

M.R.

WENDOVER

TO

Verney Junc.

By the early 1960s the charm of this one time busy junction was in decay. The Met line had been lifted and all was overgrown and uncared for. The 'tired' looking concrete post support of station enamel sign affirms this in a way that robust cast iron does not. The very wide span lattice footbridge retains its dignity to the end.

R H G Simpson

Passengers of a railtour at Verney Junction watching and photographing a 9F 2-10-0 no 92112 on a passing train of empty mineral wagons.

R H G Simpson

With the arrival of the Met& GCR Joint Committee the relationship with the LNWR mellowed somewhat and the Bletchley - Oxford services timed trains favourably. In 1904 nine Met 'down' and 'up' trains connected with six 'down' and 'up' passing trains on the Oxford - Bletchley and Banbury branch lines. This train is one of the regular two coach bogie sets behind an '18 inch Goods' no 8560 in the 1930s when the line had become part of the LMS system.

A railtour calling at Verney Junction in the 1950s using an interesting LNER coach set with restaurant car. The former Met sidings now being utilised for the storage of condemned stock.

R H G Simpson

Verney Junction looking east on Sunday June 14, 1953. Now quite untidy but largely intact, the use of the Met line as an extended siding is evident by the distant wagons. The charm of this remote complex has always fascinated, enhanced by the rustic quality of the house built for the Station Master responsible for the business of the Met&GCR Joint Railway at the station.

Neil Sprinks

A view not often photographed from the signalbox looking towards Bletchley.

Arthur Grigg Collection

Hopefully one of these rare welcome sunny days when the world seems at peace, especially at a country station in rural Buckinghamshire where the staff take a moment to pose for the camera. We seem now to have less time for such contemplative interludes.

Arthur Grigg Collection

Winslow Road looking north towards Verney Junction. The signalman/crossing keeper was employed in the ground level building on the left. The house on the left is likely to be his accommodation. Although the station building pattern is repeated along the line north of Aylesbury the buildings in this case are situated at the end of the platform.

L & GRP

Winslow Road station looking south in the early years of the 20 century.

Author's collection

Looking south at Grandborough, a substantial country station. Those familiar with this part of the Vale would realise how remote this station was. The crossing road was not much more than a minor country lane. Possibly it served well for milk collection and horse and cattle traffic but it is difficult to imagine many passengers regularly using the station.

Mowat Collection

Looking north towards the site of Verney Junction through the sad remains of Grandborough Road station on June 16, 1957.

H C Casserley

Platform 2, the 'down' side at Quainton Road station with A class tank no 41. The impression would be that the train would continue to Verney Junction.

Milepost 92½

A Junction in the Vale
Quainton Road and Brill

After the opening of the Great Central Railway in 1899 Quainton Road station became a much busier place with the shouts of men and neighing of horses heard above the grunting and complaining of recalcitrant cattle raising dust and confusion. The bright shining squads of milk churns were noisely assembled like a regiment of guards glinting in early morning sunlight as they awaited the unfailing arrival of the long trains that paused to load and unload in their attenuated progress. Their destinations provoking the imaginings of people that never journeyed much beyond Aylesbury market or adventurously to Oxford. At that time England would still be a land of huge distances, yet to be reduced by the transport acceleration of subsequent years.

The noises would diminish in the soft light of summer evenings when the fields must be left to the gathering dusk and the passing lights of trains intensifying the weak glow of oil lit stations as they rushed through, or in the case of Brill railway moving along at the pace of country ease.

Winter was so much different in the early days of railways in the Vale. Short hours of daylight would mean long hours of darkness, a darkness that nightmares could be made of, for it would be quite dangerous to venture beyond the village confines to fall into a ditch or become caught in the mired lane rooted to deep mud so that one would have to wait for daylight to escape it. That is when the railway could be a blessing, its certain progress meant that the restrictions or privations of the season could be overcome as the trains, unlike the former road coaches and wagons, could make progress even through darkness and useless roads. What it must have been like to ride in a carriage bound for one of the cities and see the lonely dim distant light of some homestead that appeared so remote in the huge and all consuming dark is beyond the imagination of this more luminous age.

A further demand on imagination would be to think of a world with such thin lines of communication. Occasional newspapers with few illustrations surrounded by compacted columns of tiny print size, for those that could read. Otherwise it was the electric telegraph promoted by the railway, or the word of mouth of railway staff and travellers. The newspapers did have columns of local news but mainly gave notice of the birth or death of monarchs, prime ministers or imperial wars.

The Junction of Quainton Road station has a remarkable history along with many other country railway stations. The character of them was very special and it was remarkable how what had once been considered an incursion into the rustic solitude became part of it. On a disturbing scale hundreds of them closed and were razed out of existence in the 1960's which makes Quainton Road unique amongst the remaining few. The fortunate thing is that the survival of Quainton Road retains the thread of this once essential aspect of im proved social life. The role of railway stations is nowadays often overlooked but they did in effect advance the national prosperity of all with the import of things like coal for heating and cooking, movement of foodstuffs and cattle etc. at affordable prices with increased accessibility for all to integrate their business interests. Apart from this the railways provided large scale secure employment and education.

It would be another thirty years; after the crises and trials of another terrible war, before another railway authority, British Railways, would decide that the main line of the proud Great Central Railway would close also, north of Claydon Junction, this took place in 1966.

Thus it was that the station of Quainton Road survived for a time as the line was used by traffic to the brickworks at Calvert just north of there. There was also some use by freight movement over the Verney Junction line to Bletchley. This however was finally closed in 1967.

Fortunately in 1969 Quainton Road was taken over by the London Railway Preservation Society that later became the Quainton Railway Society. The period of tenure of this Society has now become the longest in single ownership.

In that time it has been respectfully maintained to the praise and pleasure of visitors, never excessively, but retaining something of the appearance it would have had in its finest years.

It was joined by a building rescued from oblivion in Oxford in 1999 that is itself an important development in architectural engineering. This is the former terminus station of the Buckinghamshire Railway at Oxford of 1851. This building is a unique experience in a different way with its cast iron columns and wrought iron roof trusses and as one enters it there is an obvious visual appraisal of a creation of the Victorian age. It is now called the Visitor Centre at Quainton and with the potted palms and gleaming period coaches it is a visual delight.

Easy to imagine the tall-hatted gents and bell skirted ladies of that age strolling along its platform with clouds of portmanteau period steam catching the yellow gaslight.

The Brill Tramway

The station at Quainton Road came about in its present location as a result of the country house at Wotton Underwood of the Duke of Buckingham who was a keen railway enthusiast. He decided that he would like to have a railway to serve his estates. After the harvest of 1871 he employed his land workers on building a railway of four miles to the house. It was built under a Light Railway Order. It not only served his brick and tile works but also carried milk along the line to Quainton station and brought coal to the house to improve the benefits thereof. It was restricted to 12 mph built of light bridge rail track of 28lb per yard.

As a shareholder of the A&BR he was able to force the railway to survey its line further west to allow him to build his railway over most of his own land. Had this not been the case the railway would have taken the natural route through Pitchcott Gap placing the station well east of Quainton village and may have had another name. However he secured only a small portion of land from Winwood Charity Trust before proceeding west alongside the road leading to Quainton village which joins the A41. At this junction a station called first of all Waddesdon was built. The line then passed by the side of a house that is still there and crossed the fields with another station at Westcott. After leaving Westcott the line became more remote when it arrived at the only station on a severe curve at Wotton for the Duke's house.

The opening of the Great Central line in 1899 had its problems with the Metropolitan at Quainton Road, so in alliance with the GWR it built a connecting line from Grendon

continued on page 17

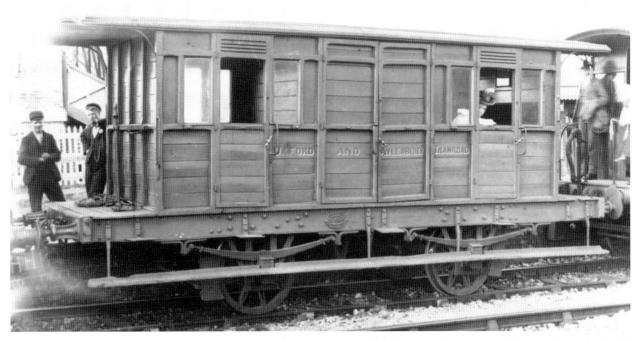

A view of the original Wotton Tramway composite passenger vehicle at Quainton Road circa 1890. The body was removed from is base in 1911 and used as a store at Brill. A replica was constructed at the Buckinghamshire Railway Centre and is in the Museum there.

Locomotive Publishing Co no 5192

One of the Aveling Porter 'locomotives' at the Buckinghamshire Railway Centre. It is part of the London Transport Museum Collection. Note the heavy chain drive that gave it the nickname from the locals 'Old Chainey' as it could be heard approaching from quite a distance.

Bill Simpson

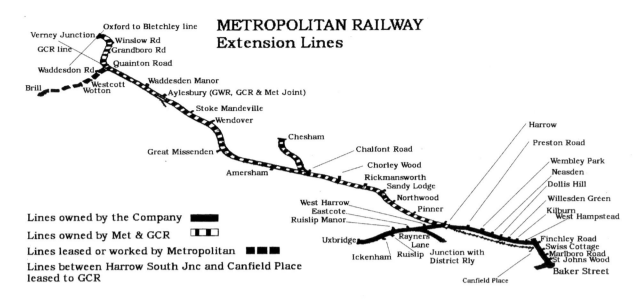

METROPOLITAN RAILWAY
Extension Lines

Oxford to Bletchley line
Verney Junction
Winslow Rd
GCR line
Grandboro Rd
Quainton Road
Waddesdon Rd
Waddesden Manor
Brill
Westcott
Wotton
Aylesbury (GWR, GCR & Met Joint)
Stoke Mandeville
Wendover
Chesham
Great Missenden
Chalfont Road
Amersham
Chorley Wood
Rickmansworth
Sandy Lodge
West Harrow
Northwood
Eastcote
Pinner
Ruislip Manor
Uxbridge
Rayners Lane
Ickenham
Ruislip
Junction with District Rly
Canfield Place

Harrow
Preston Road
Wembley Park
Neasden
Dollis Hill
Willesden Green
Kilburn
West Hampstead
Finchley Road
Swiss Cottage
Marlboro Road
St Johns Wood
Baker Street

Lines owned by the Company
Lines owned by Met & GCR
Lines leased or worked by Metropolitan
Lines between Harrow South Jnc and Canfield Place leased to GCR

The extended lines north on the Metropolitan.

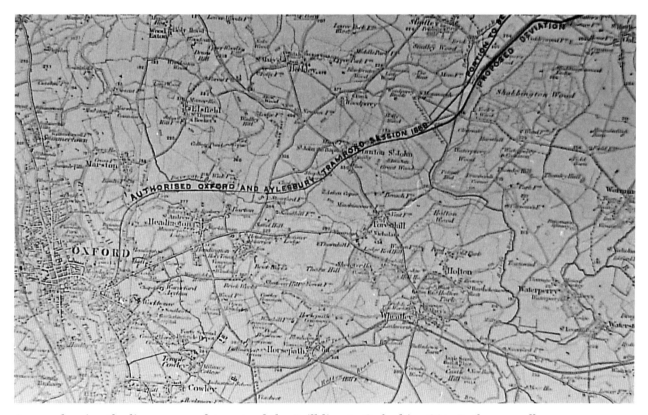

A map showing the line proposed to extend the Brill line to Oxford in 1883. Rather grandly a company was formed called the Oxford, Aylesbury & Metropolitan Junction Railway in 1882, a total distance of 23 miles absorbing the tramway. As duplication of the line from Princes Risborough to Oxford and Bletchley to Oxford it was viewed with disfavour. It was backed by Sir Harry Verney and Baron Ferdinand de Rothschild and the Metropolitan Railway paid for the survey. External pressure and the hilly terrain mitigated against the favour of capital and it failed. The Tramway was eventually taken over for operation in 1894 by the Oxford & Aylesbury Tramway with the same objective, extending the existing tramway line. That also remained unfulfilled. Had the Metropolitan seriously become involved it raises an intriguing thought upon it reaching to Oxford. Given that the Met& GCR Joint Committee effectively took up running the tramway. To do this they had to install bull-head rail but the effect of the duke's less than assiduously engineered trackbed plagued the riding on the line until its closure.

Buckinghamshire County Records

A Railway World magazine railtour in the 1950s calling at Quainton Road station hauled by L48 E class tank with a rake of Metropolitan coaches. The wagons in the background siding emphasise the intensive use of Quainton Road for goods movements, shunting stock between London and the Great Central line destinations north plus, via Claydon Junction, to access Oxford - Bletchley cross-country line.

 Southern Merchant Navy class 'Elder Dempster Line' passing the Metropolitan design signalbox at Quainton Road. The train is a LCGB special called the 'Great Central Rail Tour' that ran on September 7, 1966 shortly before the line's closure. When, with much regret to the London Railway Preservation Society, the signalbox was demolished as the Society purchased the station site.

Quite rare glimpse of one of the K class 2-6-4 tank engines on a goods train work on a siding at Quainton Road station at 3.50 pm on November 16, 1935.

G E Penny/Barry Tucker Collection

Former Metropolitan Railway 2-6-4 tank no 111, K class in 1933. Believed to be shunting at one of the stations north of Aylesbury.

Barry Tucker Collection

Underwood to Ashendon Junction this crossed close by the Tramway at Wotton on plate girder bridge. It opened in April 1906 with a new station that could never have been economically viable. This newcomer must have imposed a very different kind of railway to this area of rustic seclusion.

The villagers of Brill approached the Duke to extend his railway to the benefit of the village, which he did in 1872. The action also expanded the potential of the small brickworks established in Brill that increased into a factory sized

undertaking. It also allowed the village to market is milk output to London and of course provided the much prized import of coal. Such was the difference a railway station could make to a community.

Drivers on the Tramway always complained of its rough riding. The Duke had planned to have it horse drawn but the poor laying of the track made this beyond the horses. The introduction of the Aveling Porter converted traction engines must have been very much a

continued on page 20

The Aylesbury to Verney Junction push-pull train en route for the latter destination at platform 2 Quainton Road station hauled by ex-GER 2-4-2 tank engine no 8307. This engine and coach operated the line as a branch from Aylesbury in the 1920s and 1930s.

Barry Tucker Collection

Waddeson Road station c1930 on the Brill branch run by the Metropolitan & LNER Joint Committee, shortly to be LT. The A class no 23 is now preserved in the LTM Collection. One of the early Ashbury stock coaches provides braking for the train with its cattle wagon. The house behind remains on the site to the present day on the A41 Aylesbury - Bicester road, although the angle of the road junction has been changed.

Barry Tucker Collection

A few moments pause at Waddesdon Road station with a train composing of one of the later Metropolitan coaches. The casual air of small country stations is evident, quite a contrast for the locomotive from its Inner Circle days.

Barry Tucker Collection

A class engine no 41 approaching Westcott station.

Barry Tucker Collection

Westcott station that abutted onto the village road with the siding extended down the village street to supply the gasworks in a field on the Waddeson Manor estate.

Barry Tucker Collection

Wescott railway station, the shed with the bulging walls was probably what passed for a goods shed. By contrast the station house building is quite substantial looking with the recessed tablets in the gables one 'B&C' which abbreviates 'Buckingham & Chandos', titles of the Duke of Buckingham. In the second '1871' when the station opened. The timber on the left filled with earth and supported by banking is the stop at the end of the siding to protect the road.

TfL from the London Transport Museum Collection

half-measure, traction engines are not railway locomotives and there was only room for one man to stand in the space behind the boiler whilst the other would stand on a footboard alongside the wheels. A second man was needed for the crossings and to assist the driver. These two 0-4-0s were also fractious if they were given too great a load and would lift up their front wheels off the track.

A solution was found with more conventional Manning Wardle 0-6-0 ST engines displaced from building contractors lines. Three of these

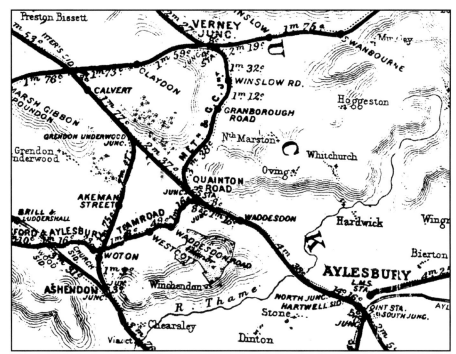

Layout of lines and distances in the area of the Vale of Aylesbury after the grouping. Note the siding for Hartwell House which was probably for coal. Note the lower level near Oving where the railway would have originally passed through Pitchcott Gap if the Duke had not insisted otherwise.

The typical train assembly of an Oxford & Aylesbury Railway train at the Brill station platform behind engine 'Brill No 1'. The man closest to the spectacle plate on the footplate is Harry Cross who was the regular driver on the branch for many years. He lived at Brill but enjoyed public houses at both ends of the line! After leaving the branch the engine was seen in 1924 working on the building of the Great West Road still with its nameplate. As it was dealing with contractors wagons it was fitted with dumb buffers. A roughly built engine shed was constructed whilst the engine was working on the temporary railway.

were bought by the Oxford & Aylesbury Railway the grandly titled new company that took over the running of the line in 1892 but never realised the objective of its title. These lasted until the Metropolitan took up the running of the branch in 1899.

After rebuilding the line with conventional bullhead rail they introduced a New D class engine, without success, so they retained the MWs to run the line until the A class engines became displaced from their work south of Harrow in 1905-10. Drivers commented that even with their flexible wheelbase riding the branch was llke being on a rocking horse.

The locomotive shed at the Brill terminus. Note the point lever on the right that controlled the roads dividing into the station loop.

Barry Tucker Collection

Wood Siding between Wotton and Brill stations on the branch. This lonely outpost at a minor road junction was manned by one member of staff. As there is no sign of any chimney it follows that it would not be a comfortable staffing duty in winter. The bridge carries the Brill line and road over the GWR line built in 1910 from Princes Risborough to Aynho Junction.

Barry Tucker Collection

One of the A class engines approaching the Brill station platform. The buildings are, from left to right, the original loco shed for the Aveling Porter engines of Wotton Tramway days. The Forge which typifies vernacular building style in the Brill district, and the locomotive shed built by the Oxford & Aylesbury Tramway for the larger engines. A favourable comparison can be made with the tramway engine shed in original 'Thomas the Tank Engine' books.

Barry Tucker Collection

The view towards the terminus end and the distant Muswell Hill that proved such an obstacle to extending the line beyond to Oxford. The coach is of early Met vintage regularly used on the Tramway. Its outside radial axles were probably tested to the limit on the extreme curve at Wotton station.

Barry Tucker Collection

How remarkably different the area north of Aylesbury once was in this view from some time in the 1930s. One of the Robinson tank engines is heading south with a train of LNER coaches.

QRS Collection

An ex-Great Eastern tank engine brings in the push-pull train from Verney Junction into Waddesdon in the 1930s. Note the use of attaching a cattle wagon behind the engine.

TfL from the London Transport Museum Collection

A GWR train arrives at Aylesbury from the south into the Joint station in what seems to be a day of some activity with all smartly attired as if on a Sunday outing.

A C Payne

The Journey South

Aylesbury

The Aylesbury of the mid nineteenth century was quite a modest affair, an extended village in effect, that was until it replaced Buckingham as the principal county town, but unlike Buckingham, Aylesbury very quickly got itself onto the rail network of that time with the opening of the Aylesbury Railway in 1839. This was a branch connection to the what later became the West Coast main line at Cheddington built by the London & Birmingham Railway. Although you had to change trains there and it was something of a minor station, but until the GWR arrived at Aylesbury from Princes Risborough in 1863 it was a unique advantage.

The GWR came as a rival to the later owners of the Aylesbury Railway, the London & North Western Railway, when they built their own station at Aylesbury. Luckily for the line to Verney Junction (A&BR) they obliged not only to make a connection in this new station but to run trains for them as they were too broke to run their own.

The LNWR fumed at the parsimonious little railway finding a big brother to help them out in trying to connect with their own line from Oxford to Bletchley at the newly rebuilt Verney Junction. There it stood, solitary among its lonely fields where the LNWR resisted to time its own trains to meet the rival Swindon locomotive hauled trains from Aylesbury. They wanted everybody to go to and from Aylesbury via Cheddington.

However, there was more than one big brother on the horizon, as another route to London took form with the Metropolitan Railway's probe north with Edward Watkin as its standard bearer. The Metropolitan bought the A&BR and formed a Joint Committee with the southern venturing of the Great Central Railway where they joined north of Quainton Road Station. Thus Verney Junction station was capaciously rebuilt by the Joint Committee.

The locomotive shed at Aylesbury was rebuilt along with the main station building upon the formation of the Met&GCR Joint Committee. From the origins of the original shed it was shared with the GWR for purposes seen here of the Princes Risborough to Aylesbury push-pull train service.

Andrew Bratton

One of the 'Dreadnought' coaches at Aylesbury in London Transport days.

H C Casserley

Standard tank no 80117 with a train bound for Amersham in the 1950s hauling the LT 'Dreadnought' coaches. It awaits the progress of former LNER V2 in the main line platform. Note the white bands painted around the water column that was done to sight this during the wartime blackout.

H C Casserley

A southbound train hauled by one of the L1 tank engines no 67772. The class took over the workings of steam north of Amersham when they were handed over to the LNER by London Transport in 1933.

The view north from the footbridge at Aylesbury showing the first broad gauge good shed.

Payne & Son

The presence of the GWR at Aylesbury prevailed long after they ceased working the line to Verney Junction as they continued to operate the service to Princes Risborough. Here 2-6-2 tank engine no 3906 at the Joint locomotive shed on March 15, 1930. An interesting deviation on the Churchward generation of tank engines that was a development from a William Dean 0-6-0 of 1896. They were rebuilt as such in 1907. Modellers note the crane behind used for coaling engines.

H C Casserley

Stoke Mandeville station looking north. There was an undeniable elegance about the stations on the northern section of the Metropolitan.

H C Casserley

Through the Chilterns
Stoke Mandeville to Harrow

It is two miles south of Aylesbury to Stoke Mandeville station. Nevertheless it is well patronised and possibly providential for the famous hospital. The single coal siding that was looped on the 'up' side was removed in 1968.

Although a station was built north of Aylesbury for Waddesdon Manor a family of greatest influence in the Vale of Aylesbury and beyond from the middle of the nineteenth century and into the twentieth was the Rothschilds. The banking magnates built houses all around the district beginning near Cheddington with Mentmore, which is now unoccupied. Another house called Tring Park has now become a school for performing arts. Halton House was sold to the RAF. It was used by the army during the First World War. Aston Clinton had a varied existence as a wartime hospital and school until it was demolished in 1956-8. Ascott House was given to the National Trust, as was Waddesdon Manor. They had owned forty stately houses across England and Europe. The land for Waddesdon Manor was purchased from the Duke of Marlborough.

At the time (1874) Baron Ferdinand Rothschild remarked that the nearest station was at Aylesbury. Obviously he did not consider the A&BR station at Quainton Road to be of any useful importance. Part of his reasoning for building the house was that he believed that in four years it would have contact with Baker Street by a direct line. Obviously he did not consider the GWR line through Princes Risborough to be adequate.

A water problem was overcome by a water company at Aylesbury that drew from the Chiltern Hills so the baron laid down seven miles of pipes to connect not only the house but the village with a water supply which must have been to its enormous gratification as local springs had always been susceptible to drought.

continued on page 33

Wendover station looking north. The railway to the Halton Camp left from the distant goods yard.

H C Casserley

One of the ex-GCR tank engines a Robinson 4-6-2 in LNER livery no 5024 passing through Stoke Mandeville in the 1930s.

H C Casserley

Stanier tank engine no 42231 on a southbound train at Wendover.

H C Casserley

One of the Fowler tank engines of Bournville shed seen here near Great Missenden on May 10, 1958 with an 'up' train.

H C Casserley

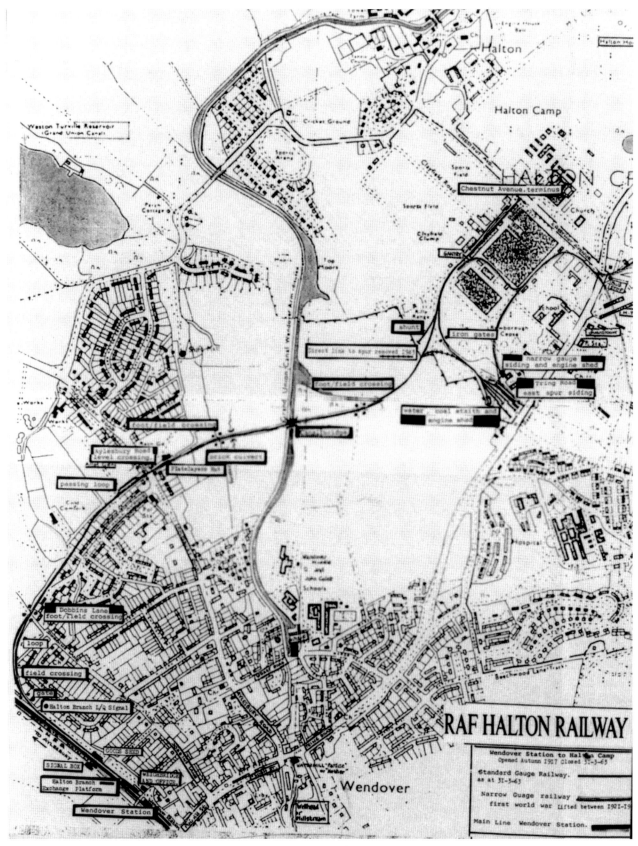

Layout of the railway that ran into RAF Halton from Wendover station.

Museum Collection RAF Halton

An H class Jones 4-4-4T no 110 looking immaculate on an Amersham - Aylesbury train passing through the Chilterns.

RAS

Mature trees were moved and replanted with roots enclosed in balls of earth. To manage such enormous weight must have been a prodigious task.

The influence of their enormous wealth provided employment in the Vale and supported suppliers of goods and services. This included the railway to which they contributed for an additional station for the Manor which opened in 1897. A House warming was held at Waddesdon in July 1883. It had taken only four years to build aided by the Tramway carrying much material, its towers and pinnacles rising on the top of Lodge Hill in a French style which gave it an architectural distinction like a kind of Xanadu overlooking Quainton Road station. In deference to this the Rothschilds did provide instant tree cover by planting mature trees. Also the Manor received many evacuated children in trains from the east end of London in 1939. It is still popularly appreciated by many visitors each year retaining in all its grandeur the affinity of the Rothschild name in the district.

Baron Ferdinand bequeathed on the village a hotel, a village hall with reading room, plus temperance and benefit societies. He expressed delight that the Metropolitan Railway had joined the Great Central Railway and furnished a station 'not a mile from the park gates'. This saved a tedious six miles or so drive to Aylesbury.

Queen Victoria visited Waddesdon May 14, 1890. She travelled from Windsor to Aylesbury on the GWR.

Wendover

Wendover brings the line into the area most typical of the rolling countryside of the Chilterns. The station situated west of the town has lost its exclusive sylvan prospect now by being joined alongside with a by-pass (A413) road that was added in 1998

Wendover was the station for the former Rothschild house at Halton.

It was requested as an appropriate position to encamp divisions of the British Expeditionary Force at the outbreak of the first World War. Alfred de Rothschild conceded to this and continued his support by also allowing the early formations of the Royal Flying Corps to have a permanent camp on the site. This was built by Sir Robert McAlpine. The house was eventually made over to the permanent use of the service.

An H class no 106 leaving Chalfont station in the 1920s with an ex-Chesham train bound for Baker Street.
R K Blencowe

One of the mighty K class no 115 undertaking the duties for which it was intended handling one of the Metropolitans not inconsiderable freight trains at Chalfont in the 1920s.
H C Casserley

Former Great Central locomotive LNER 6168 'Lord Stuart of Wortley'. It was built in 1920, converted to B3/2 in 1929, then withdrawn in 1946. It is seen here passing over Joint metals with a train through the Chilterns.

H C Casserley

To serve the camp a railway was built from the sidings at the station to the camp by the Metropolitan using German pow labour this was 1¾ miles in length and went from the north end of the station yard. A collection of industrial locomotives were employed to run this line onto the camp. A narrow gauge system was also built on the camp (see a History of the Metropolitan vol. 2 by Bill Simpson).

The Camp continued after the war and became a training school for the Royal Air Force for which it continues at the present time. The camp railway was overtaken by road use and closed on March 31. 1963.

Amersham

London Transport announced electrification of Rickmansworth to Amersham and Chesham in 1937, however the intervention of the war deferred this.

A town in two parts as Old Amersham situated at the bottom of the hill where the Church dates from the 13 century. Whereas Amersham-on-the-Hill developed after the arrival of the railway on the higher ground opening on September 1, 1892. Which like other stations on the line makes it a rather late inclusion to the railway map.

The Metropolitan Country Estates purchased the Weller Estate of 78 acres in 1930 to cover it with 535 semi-detached houses with 51 shops. Thus providing the nucleus of the new Amersham and promoting the concept of 'Metroland'.

Electrification of the line however was somewhat late arriving from Rickmansworth to Amersham due the interruption of the war. In 1960 work began on the £9,000,000 scheme to electrify from Rickmansworth to Amersham to be completed in September 11, 1961. This involved four tracking from Harrow on the Hill to Watford south junction. Also the widening of 13 bridges.

Metropolitan line services were withdrawn on September 10, 1961 from north of Amersham. In effect this then became the electronic terminus as it was never considered economically justified to proceed beyond. Should the plans for the nascent East-West-Rail ever consider electrifying the line from Claydon Junction to Aylesbury there would then be a gap between two power delivery systems.

Early photograph of an A class tank no 17 with a Chesham bound train. This would be the original form without cab and the raised numbers on the chimney front. Note steam rising from the chimney over the water tank which proves the problem of condensing when the water got very hot in the side tanks. This locomotive was listed with the name 'Ixion'. It was withdrawn in 1907.

R K Blencowe

Chalfont and Latimer and Chesham

The railway opened to Chesham on July 8, 1889. The four mile branch was worked by electric tablet, but in 1949 the single line was track circuited and colour light signals installed. This enabled the branch to be worked without token; the signals at one end automatically locking with those at the other end. Electric trains ran to Chesham first of all on August 15, 1960 using multiple unit T stock with some trains of electric locomotives hauling the Aylesbury stock which could use the run-round at Chesham. This enabled the service to include an extra twenty trains a day. The last day of the steam shuttle was on September 11, 1960. The familiar ex-GCR C13 67418 being supplanted by one of the Ivatt 2-6-2 tanks 41284. The goods workings on the branch ceased in 1966 whilst one of the platforms ceased use in 1970.

Rickmansworth

Rickmansworth became identified with the failed northern advance of the Metropolitan with its electrification being prevented by war. As it had arrived from Harrow on January 5, 1925. Together with the LNER it opened to Watford on November 2 of the same year. Rickmansworth became noted for the organisation and dexterity of the railway staff. Thus it was that passengers could observe the skilful procedure of interchange between steam and electric on trains going north and south. The practised skill was completed in under five minutes so that most passengers deep in their morning or evening papers would hardly know that it had been completed.

Converted motorised set at Chalfont on July 23, 1955.

H C Casserley

One of the Ivatt 2-6-2 tanks on the Chesham shuttle on January 3, 1959. The ample evidence of condensing steam suggests a seasonably cool day. The train consists of converted motorised stock that would only be able to run independently from Rickmansworth to London.

R M Casserley

The one surviving steamable Met locomotive engine No 1 seen here at Chesham on April 22, 1933.

H C Casserley

The E class L48 at Chesham on June 3, 1956 with the 'John Milton Special' from Crystal Palace with a train made up of Metropolitan compartment stock. The train was also hauled by electric locomotives 'Thomas Lord' and 'Benjamin Disraeli' calling at New Cross Gate over St Mary's curve between Shadwell and Aldgate East over the Metropolitan line to Rickmansworth where the E class took over and carried the train over the Chesham branch and back.

H C Casserley

MetroVick locomotive no 5 'John Hampden' with an Aylesbury train of Dreadnought stock on April 22, 1933 at Rickmansworth. It would at this point be released to be replaced with steam.

H C Casserley

Stanier tank engine no 42588 with the 12.35 Aylesbury to Liverpool Street train at Rickmansworth on January 3, 1959.

R M Casserley

Two MetroVick locos in position to take southbound trains in the Rickmansworth goods yard.

RAS

The original Metropolitan & Great Central Joint Committee station at Watford with on of the 1905 stock trains on June 10, 1939. A fine sunny day at the station amongst tree lined villas. Sad to think of such a perfect English scene to be overshadowed by a terrible war. Note the cattle facility usage at the station and end loading dock.

Photo G K Kerley

Chesham branch terminus with exGCR 4-4-2 tank engine C13 no 67418 of British Railways Eastern Region.
John H Meredith

Chalfont & Latimer station on July 23, 1955 with the north bound train being hauled by no 67416 a C13 4-4-2T on Saturday, a through train to Chesham from Liverpool Street. On the left a pleasant period feel of the coaches in the Chesham branch bay.

H C Casserley

A London Transport train on December 12, 1937 with the 12.41 pm Wembley Park to Chesham seen leaving Wembley Park behind former Metropolitan Electric locomotive No 15 'Wembley Exhibition 1924' hauling standard steam stock.

G E Penny/Barry Tucker Collection

Harrow to Baker Street

Harrow

The station opened in 1880 with the extension of the Met line north from Willesden Green on August 2. As electrification moved further north Harrow became the next change over point for electric/steam trains after Willesden Green. Expansion began early but after electrification more so as it became the centre of a deeply populous suburb of north London with the growth extending along the Uxbridge branch to places like Rayners Lane.

The Uxbridge branch opened on July 4, 1904 and was worked by steam for six months at the beginning. A dream of Metropolitan Estates Committee of the expansion of property owning commuters on season tickets became realised. This fortitude was also dipped into by the Metropolitan & District Railway from March 1, 1910.

In 1961 2¾ miles of trackbed widening took place quadrupling tracks north of Harrow for the benefit of British Railways and fast Metropolitan Line trains to avoid stations used by the stopping trains service.

Neasden

Neasden remains to this day a significant depot for storing and maintaining London Transport stock. The Metropolitan moved from the steam shed situated at Edgware Road station in 1910 as the Circle became largely steam free. The extension of the line north to that point came in 1880. The name became synonymous with the rail complex and the building of the power station that opened in 1905. The needs of electric power becoming paramount for the expanding railway. The power station closed in 1968 and was subsequently demolished in 1969. Neasden steam shed closed in 1937 following on as part of the LT New Works scheme of 1935-40 which included a large new depot on the former locomotive works and carriage shed site at Neasden. Steam locomotive power was to be eliminated from the former Met under this programme.

The working of steam north of Rickmansworth and freight working was passed to the LNER on November 1, 1937. Consequently Met locos were handed over for this work but they retained thirteen for engineer's train duties.

The first train from Baker Street to Harrow hauled by the ubiquitous A class in 1880.
J Whittenbury/Railway Magazine

Baker Street Grade II

As one might expect Baker Street station has a very distinctive architectural design from other underground stations. Emphasising its significance as an important junction on the Underground. From here one could depart from the Circle to the wooded slopes of 'Metroland'. It is of course a place of great haste, as one would expect, but the style is impressive.

The tiled faience geometry with roundels sets off the ornate lettering of former shop usage. It suggests style influence between the art nouveau and art deco. The once graciously ornate Chiltern Court above, now converted to flats, recalls memories of fronded palms and reflections in bevelled glass. Surrounding diners in the genteel surroundings compared to the rushing world outside. A regular operation carried out was the siding in the station where coal delivery trains reversed in for Chiltern Court.

Baker Street station is still confident in its period whatever the ephemeral confusion of tastes may be imposed in the streets beyond. The first station was designed by Sir John Fowler, Engineer in charge of the Metropolitan

Railway. What is seen today is from the extensive remodelling in 1911-13 by Charles W Clark, Chief Architectural Assistant to the Engineer Mr W Willox. With the building of Chiltern Court above, completed in 1929, the original lunettes for light and ventilation were concealed. By now electrification had removed the steam smoke problem. The attraction of this one time essential feature was effectively restored with electric lighting in the remodelling of 1985.

An outstanding General Manager and Director of the Metropolitan who joined it in 1903 was R H Selbie who held office until his death on May 17, 1930. During his period of office women had become employed on the Met as guards and gatemen.

The railway was absorbed into the London Passenger Transport Board at its formation in 1933.

That continued until 1948 when it became the London Transport Executive, which was under the administration of the British Transport Commission.

This ceased in 1962 when it became London Transport Underground Limited 1985-2003. Transport for London from 2003 onwards to the present day.

Aylesbury to Baker Street train Met E class 0-4-4 tank loco no 80 in 1934 with standard steam stock. The locomotive was withdrawn in 1963.

by G E Penny/Barry Tucker Collection

The fiftieth Anniversary of the opening of the branch from Harrow to Uxbridge, took place on June 30, 1904. The locomotive that hauled that train, Met 1 0-4-4 E class tank was able to revisit the line to perform the same duty on June 30, 1954.

H C Casserley

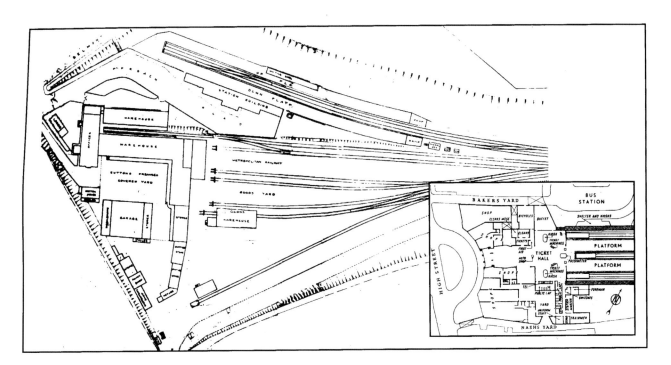

The terminus at Uxbridge (inset detail) that was built after the extension from the original station that opened in December 1938.

London Transport, Neasden with 1905 clerestory roofed electric corridor train leaving Neasden car sheds on September 7, 1937.

G E Penny/Barry Tucker Collection

The new shed at Neasden built by London Transport with one of the Peckett saddletanks in steam and an A class L45.

H C Casserley

The Neasden 'Flaggy'. A duty flagman that attended the crossing at Neasden works September 9, 1937.

Barry Tucker Collection

Metropolitan Railway Neasden Electric power house 6/9/37 . The station opened in 1904 and closed in 1968. These were the early days of the power supply industry when it was fragmented in its development to customised requirements. An Act of 1926 established a Central Electricity Generating Board, in other words the formation of the national grid. The District Railway was supplied from Lots Road power station that generated power from 1905 until 2002. Its profile with two huge chimneys provided moody smoke misty illustrations along the banks of the River Thames.

G E Penny/Barry Tucker Collection

Metropolitan Railway Neasden Sheds for housing of special saloon, breakdown train, signal and petrol vans and frost scraping trains September 14, 1937.

G E Penny/Barry Tucker Collection

Metropolitan Railway, Neasden Steam locomotive shed, the three roads occupied by no 97 G class 2-6-4T engine 'Brill' and K class tank no 113.

G E Penny/Barry Tucker Collection

An LNER train on Sunday December 12, 1237. It departed Quainton Road at 11.15 am for Marylebone and is seen now approaching Wembley Park station. The locomotive is LNER (exGCR) 4-6-2 tank no 5448, a Robinson design of 1911, express suburban tank that operated out of Marylebone until the late 1940's. Some of the class lingered into the late 1950s.

G E Penny/Barry Tucker Collection

The summer 1904 and the progress of a Neasden stopping train between Willesden Green and what is now Dollis Hill station (not then built) 0-4-4 E class tank engine no 78 with a train of six eight-wheel (non bogie) coaches. The first class coaches have cream upper panels. A photograph by H G Ammand from the window of house no 261 Chapter Road, Willesden Green.

H G Ammand

The early style of the Metropolitan railway stations is retained in the buildings of the original Marlborough Road station that served after closing, as a restaurant.

Bill Simpson

Some crinkly roof tiles replaced the originals which adds interest to the plain lines of the entrance to Wembley Park Station. The crested raised sections between the overhanging canopies were once tall chimneys that have been cut and capped.

Bill Simpson

The new Metropolitan station frontage at Bayswater shortly after completion.

Railway Gazette

In the City

The first underground railway in the world grew out of overwhelming necessity. The solution for the crowded streets in 1830 was to build a new road from Farringdon Street, from Ludgate Circus to Holborn Hill, this was opened in that year. Powers to extend this north to Clerkenwell Green came in 1838 this was at the same time as the London to Birmingham main line was opened. This was followed with the opening of the Great Western Railway to Bristol in 1841. The Great Northern Railway to York in 1850, Shoreditch 1840, Fenchurch Street in 1841, Nine Elms in 1838 and Waterloo in 1848; whilst the London & Greenwich Railway had brought in 6 million passengers by 1840.

Clearly the impending progress of the large railway companies to access the capital with mass transit was not waiting on deliberations of the City Corporation that sought through financial astringency to fund the need for new roads and act on the powers gained. Thereby progress would be too slow for the gradual sticking plaster solution of piecemeal building of new roads. A greatly expanded London never finds a total solution at any time, in the 21st century a congestion charge was applied to ease the problem. In the early nineteenth century the streets were clogged with horse traffic that must have had them smelling like a farmyard. Add to that the sound of iron rimmed wheels running on cobbles and it must have been almost impossible to speak in areas were the traffic managed to gather some pace.

However this was the age of the railway and a champion of this new transport system was the solicitor to the Corporation of the City of London one Charles Pearson who took up his position in 1839. He was sure that an underground railway would solve the problem quicker but it had to be progressed before areas became built over and it became practically impossible to construct it.

Proposal schemes were drawn up that included a complete restoration of the Valley of the River Fleet, which by all accounts had become a mess of insanitary precipitation and likely to infect its miasma throughout the city. So the railway would achieve greater benefit by dealing with this.

In the midst of his plans a Great Exhibition for Science and Industry was to open in Hyde Park in 1851 which would intensify the swelling

The Metropolitan was built with some advantages in steam driven machinery here is a steam driven lifting crane.

Railway Gazette

Kensington station under construction.

Railway Gazette

The Leinster Gardens construction that had to be concealed from the street above by a walled dummy house frontage so that it would not break the building line above.
Railway Gazette

population with regular special excursion trains entering and leaving the city.

This brought about a revised appreciation of the underground railway scheme that Pearson would not let die. An advantage to his plans was a new link road across the north of the city from the Valley of the Fleet to Kings Cross area, where the Great Northern Railway station opened in 1851. Onwards to Paddington where the Great Western Railway had opened in 1841. Further the GWR had extended their operations from Reading to Didcot and Birmingham in 1852.

The Great Western were a little more vulnerable in their remoteness compared to Euston and Kings Cross stations which were comparatively closer to the city centre. By interesting the board of the GWR Pearson was able to gain some investment for the scheme

from them. The GWR at that time was built in the 7ft ¼in gauge which by now was fortifying itself to the assailants from the rival narrow 4ft 8½in gauge in a period called 'The Gauge War'.

Thus was born the Bayswater, Paddington & Holborn Bridge Railway to be built as cut-and-cover. The first meeting of its directors took place on January 10, 1853. At a subsequent meeting on July 21, 1853 a less wordy title of North Metropolitan Railway was adopted. Thus the Bill went forward to become an Act of incorporation with the Royal Assent on August 15, 1853! A staggeringly impressive rate of progress compared to the lumbering legislation for Bills in the 21st century! The GWR agreed to subscribe £175,000 to the scheme provided it accommodated the broad gauge and ran into Paddington Yard. The Metropolitan had to pick

The Joint station frontage of Gloucester Road, a bold visual style, with Italian influence. The District Railway contractors were Peto & Betts, Keck & Waring Bros.

Railway Gazette

their way on this as the 4ft 8½in standard gauge was being forced on the broad gauge with potential schemes to join the underground so a mixed gauge solution came about to get the support of the GWR. The Metropolitan also absorbed the proposals of the City terminus scheme.

The line was laid out to be built from Paddington to the general Post Office at St Martins-le-Grand authorising a GWR subscription and further, the Great Northern Railway also secured powers to subscribe £175,000.

Unfortunately this momentum was not retained, the Crimean war and the additional fear of rail travel emphasised further by being underground did not encourage the flow of capital. In order to ensure progress a John Lewis Ricardo agreed to finance the work becoming Chairman for a few months.

Another prospectus was issued on July 15, 1856 that still did not encourage enough financial support.

Pearson was not to be dissuaded from what by now must have required his energies to the point of obsession. A public meeting was held on December 1, 1858 to remonstrate and demonstrate that which was urgently needed. Possibly the claim to provide cheap tickets for the working classes to move around may have pricked up the ears of potential investors. Thus it was that the City Corporation decided to become involved to the tune of £200,000, a considerable sum in 1859. This amounted to one fifth of the intended capital.

An Act of August 8, 1859 replaced the terminus of the Post office with Farringdon Street.

The Chief Engineer appointed for the project was one John Fowler, later Sir John, the resident Engineer being one T Marr Johnson. The Contractors, so historically portrayed in prominence with their wagons filled with great Victorian luminaries on the opening day photograph, was Smith & Knight for the section from Bishops Road to Euston Square. Thence one John Jay for the section to Victoria Street, which later became Farringdon Road in 1863.

Construction contracts were placed in 1859 When works commenced in that year a

North London streets facing the added obstruction of the excavations for building the cut and cover railway.
Railway Gazette

connection was made initially at Paddington for the removal of spoil and conveyance of materials. This was completed in August 1860.

Descriptions of the early market at Smithfield suggest a sickening gothic menage of slaughtered animals taking place in hellish alcoves with screaming beasts and rivulets of blood channels which even by nineteenth century standards needed reforming. Driving them to their fate through the streets must have been a chaotic in the least with fresh excrement adding to residual filth. A strong lobby of persuasion applied to have the market moved outside of the city but the railways' increased ability to carry previously slaughtered meat and the potential building of the underground railway gave the site new opportunities.

In 1860 City of London Corporation decided to develop the meat Market at Smithfield and the GWR and Metropolitan applied to lease the basement beneath the market. The underground complex at Smithfield market was built by the GWR in 1869. This followed the opening of the Widened Lines from Kings Cross to Moorgate. The Victorians were seldom measured with restraint and produced a building of some grandeur with its resplendent archways and

steel gating that measured 620ft by 240ft. Something of an engineering marvel was the construction of sidings, cranes and lifts for the import of meat and poultry from beneath. It was used by the GWR, Metropolitan, Midland Railway, Great Northern Railway, London & South Western Railway, London, Chatham & Dover Railway, with the northern part being owned by the Met and south part owned by the GWR. The movement of so many company's trains and shunting of locomotives suggests an organisation of staggering complexity which the Victorians seemed to revel in. The last train ran into there in 1960. It has now been developed as an underground car park.

Having begun the scheme of excavation it was essential to progress its completion without delay to be completed in 21 months. The method of 'cut and cover' a trench of 15 feet deep and 30 feet wide, beneath new roads would bring some obstruction for a time. It all took place during the summer of 1861, The first trial trip, over the line took place on May 24, 1862. Yet the Fleet River sewer was not to be concealed without protest and burst into the workings in Farringdon Street on June 18 filling them to a depth of ten feet as far as Kings Cross. After this

The capacious construction of the first sub surface stations must have proved impressive as here at Gloucester Road with the steel ribbed roofing and blind arcaded retaining walls. This would be just prior to the opening of the station.

Railway Gazette

Close by Paddington main line station the circle station of Praed Street here under construction.

Railway Gazette

The completed Praed Street station in 1868 when the GWR had resigned their interest in the Metropolitan, somewhat temporarily. Consequently at this station the track was not laid in the mixed gauge.

Railway Gazette

Some construction scenes look so precarious. The rails on the timber platform section where the men are standing suggests the steam crane in the background moves along to the edge of this to the drop down to the station roof supports, a fragment of which are just visible.

Railway Gazette

Beneath centuried towers of Westminster Abbey the District Railway section of the Inner Circle line is under construction. A great disadvantage to the District Railway was the survey which carried it beneath some of the most established built up areas near the river between South Kensington and Westminster.
Railway Gazette

was repaired another trial train ran on August 30. Rather fortunate that the ingress did not take place during the first trial run!

On Monday December 22, 1862 Colonel Yolland of the Board of Trade Railway Inspectorate made his inspection and gave his general approval upon completion of recommended changes to the block signalling. This would be completed no doubt for the following inspection on January 3, 1863 which was followed by a period of empty trains running over the line to test signalling and accustom the staff to working in the very different circumstances from a surface railway. This was done up to January 8.

From an agreement of November 1861 the GWR agreed to work the line providing motive power and rolling stock which would of course be in the broad gauge. Early drawings of the opening period show this to be the case.

On Friday, January 8 1862 some 600 guests travelled from Bishop's Road to Farringdon Street in two trains leaving at 1 pm taking 2 hours 10 minutes, no doubt stopping to inspect the impressive work undertaken en route.

The occasion was marked with the usual fete of indulgence that conspicuously marked such celebrations arranged at Farringdon Street. This was followed by the usually grandiose speeches of the triumphs over adversity which had some credibility, confirmed by the works.

The Directors granted an annuity of £250 to the widow of Charles Pearson who passed away on September 1862. He did at least see his life's work realised in its early stages.

The public had their opportunity to experience this triumph on January 10, 1863 with 67 trains on weekdays and 48 on Sundays. Unhesitatingly 40,000 were carried over the line
continued on page 75

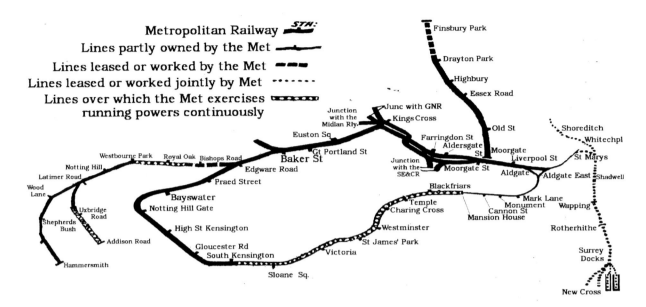

Stations of the Inner Circle and branches.

An early drawing of how the approach to Baker Street Junction looked shortly after the building of the junction.
Railway Magazine

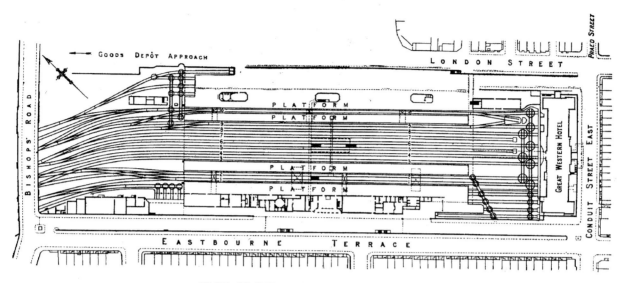

PLAN OF PADDINGTON STATION IN 1854.

Plan view of Paddington station in 1854. Much stock was moved around using horses and crossing lines over turntables.

Railway Magazine

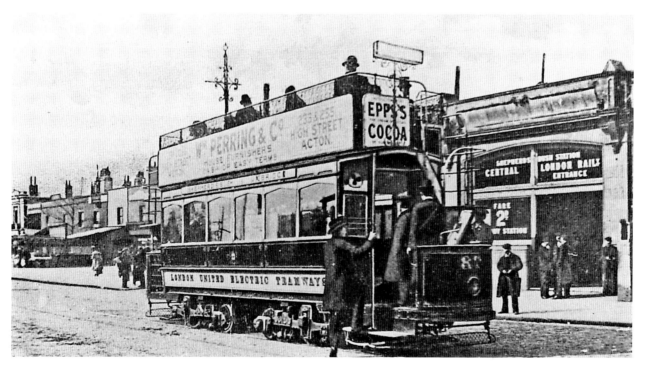

London Electric Tramways car at Shepherds Bush station of the Central London Railway. This was a terminus for lines to Hounslow and Hillingdon.

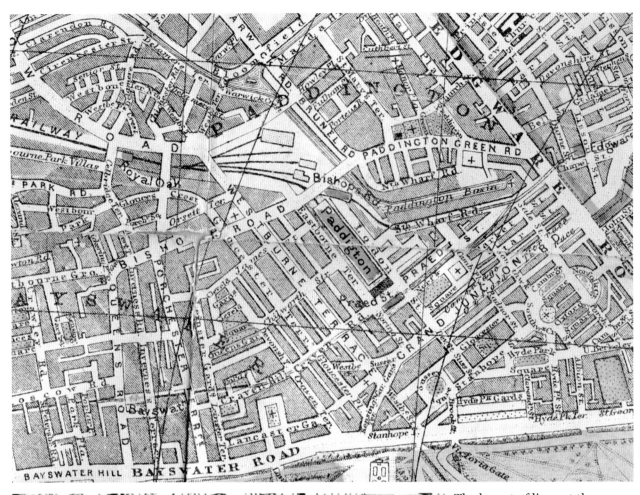

The layout of lines at the Bishops Road station in 1874 as the completion of the Inner Circle was still incomplete. Where the lines are above ground they are filled in black, beneath the ground lighter as two lines.

Authors Collection

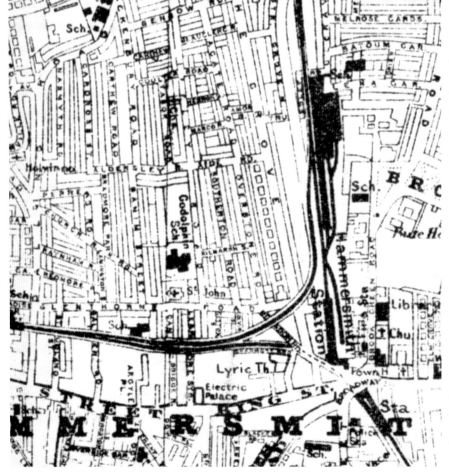

Map of Hammersmith terminus that was extended further south to open on December 1, 1868. This allowed the junction for the LSWR trains to run to Richmond from June 1, 1870, by agreement, also GWR and Metropolitan trains.

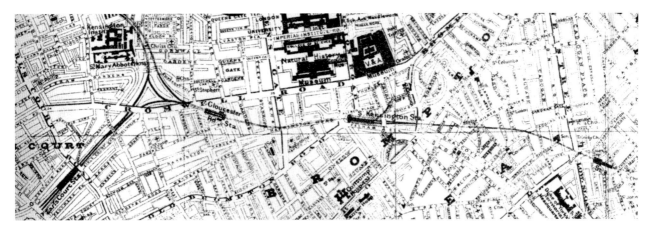

Map view of the southern part of the Inner Circle with Gloucester Road change station for journeys west on the District Railway.

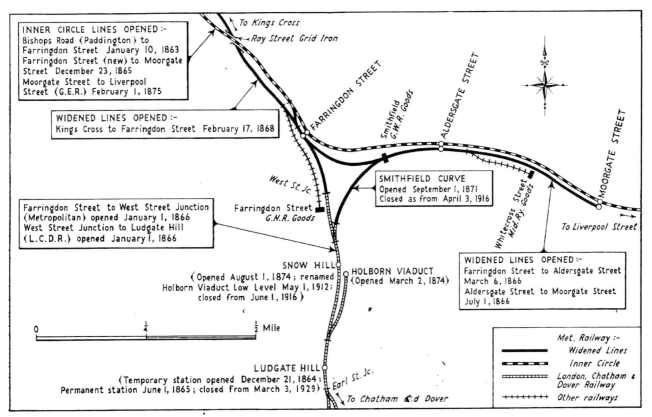

Main-line railway approaches to Moorgate Street, and north-south link, in 1914

The area of the Smithfield Curve complex in 1914.

Railway Magazine

The original Ray Street gridiron built to support the Circle line in the Widened lines development.

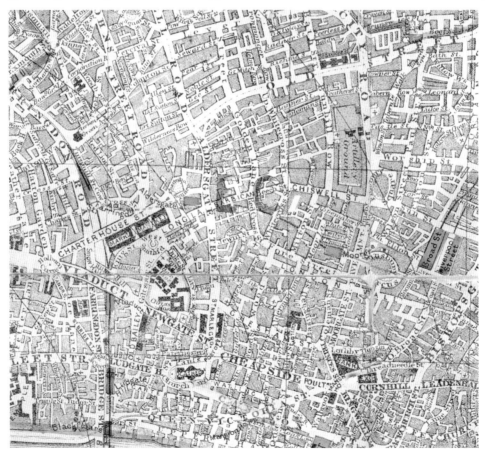

The situation at Farringdon Street in 1874 with the LCDR line going south to cross the river at Blackfriars and the Met line going round to Aldersgate and Moorgate. Note detail of the Smithfield Market the junction curve beneath the market and the horseshoe shape West Smithfield with the road access to the underground complex.
Author's Collection

One of the original cut and cover stations at Farringdon Street shows how the Underground railway retained areas of maximum light to offset the apprehension of the long steam cloudy tunnels.

Bill Simpson

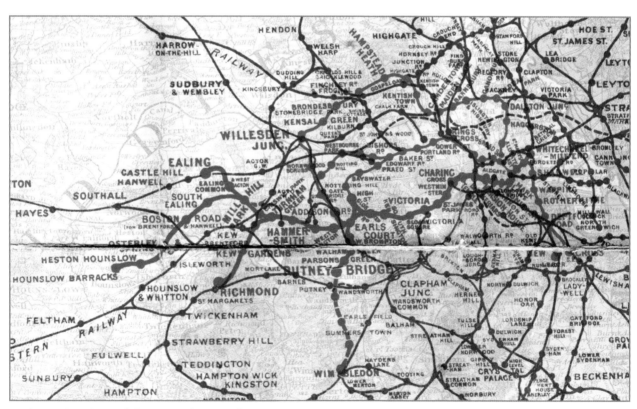

Early publications of the expanding Underground became ludicrously complex to be almost useless. Thus the superb interpretation by Harry Beck in 1934 came none too soon. The lasting inspiration of his creation must find daily appreciation by bewildered travellers.

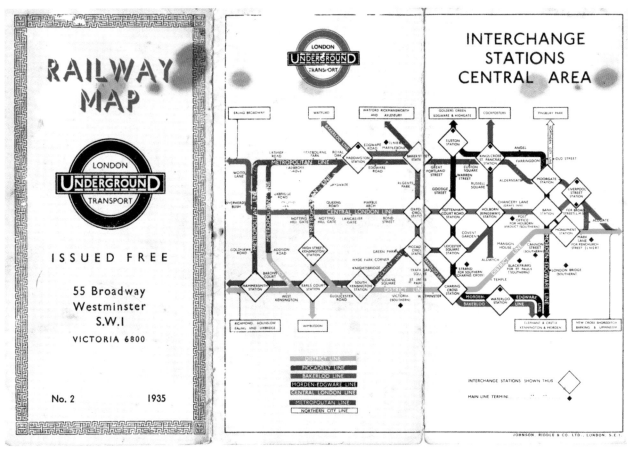

Early work of Harry Beck on a leaflet produced by London Transport in 1935. The simplification of direct information must have eased things a great deal. The Metropolitan Railway (red) & The Metropolitan & District Railway (green) lines being clearly evident.

Reproduced by kind permission of the London Transport Museum

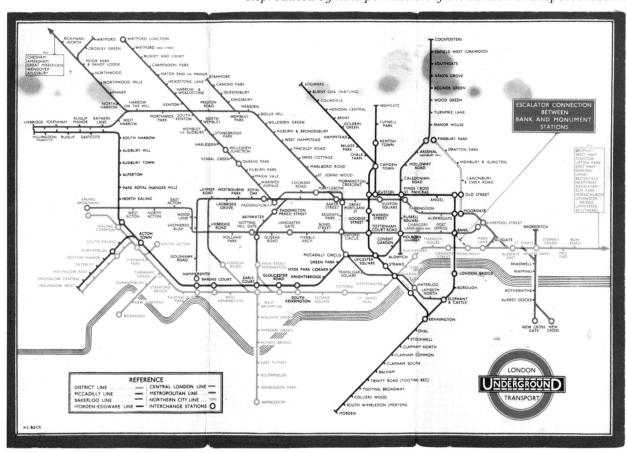

The ingenious simplification in the No. 2 issue of the map.
Reproduced by kind permission of the London Transport Museum

The Bluebell Railway fortunately recovered the former Metropolitan coaches used on the Chesham branch and they are regularly used to give some 'Metroland' experience for their visitors.

Bill Simpson

The atmosphere of Baker Street always prevails with its period architecture. No surprise that it should inspire images from Sherlock Holmes stories.

Bill Simpson

Restoration work on the preserved lines has provided experiences for visitors that would have been lost forever. For those of interest, this beautiful 4-wheel 1st class coach worked on the Kent & East Sussex Railway.

Bill Simpson

A number of GWR design pannier 0-6-0s were bought by London Transport in 1956 to replace old Met steam locos on permanent way trains and trips to Croxley Tip on the Watford branch. One of these is preserved at Quainton Road where it arrived in 1970. It is seen here on a siding there.

Bill Simpson

The preserved E class in revered preservation at the Buckinghamshire Railway Centre.

Bill Simpson

Artists impression of how the station on the Aylesbury - Quianton Road Junction called Waddesdon would have looked like in Wotton Tramway days.

Bill Simpson

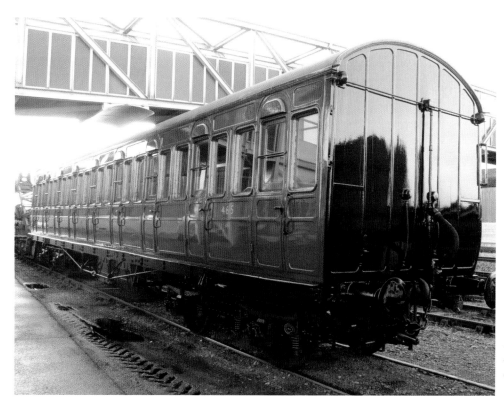

During the celebrations of 150 years of the London Underground the Quianton Railway Society hired a 'Dreadnought' coach from the Vintage Carriage Trust to run special trains at the Centre. It is seen here shortly after its arrival on a siding at Quianton.

Bill Simpson

The flair for costumed Events is often featured at the Buckinghamshire Railway Centre. This attractive young lady has entered into the spirit of things helping create a pleasant Edwardian summer day occasion alongside Metropolitan Railway engine No 1.

Bill Simpson

It is always a delight to show work created by Quainton Railway Society members and Ed Schoon has with great skill created in 7mm scale model of one of the Metropolitan coaches used on the Brill branch.

Bill Simpson

To haul Ed Schoon's coach he has also built a model of one of the Manning Wardle engines used on the branch 'Brill No 1'. The first rate paintwork and lining gives colour to monochrome illustrations of the period.

Bill Simpson

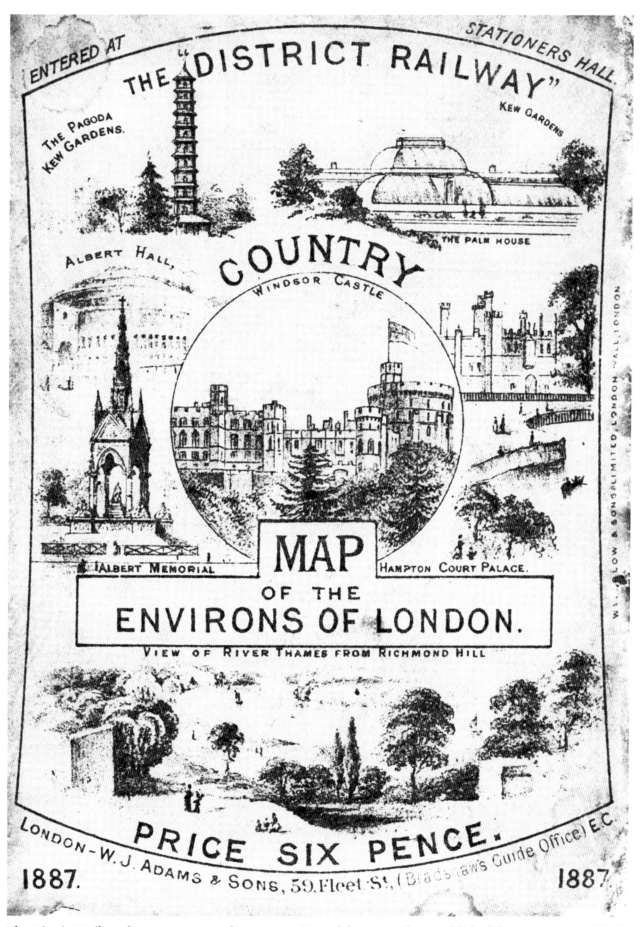

The District Railway keen to promote the opportunities of the new railway published their own maps. This is the cover of the 1887 edition.

Author's Collection

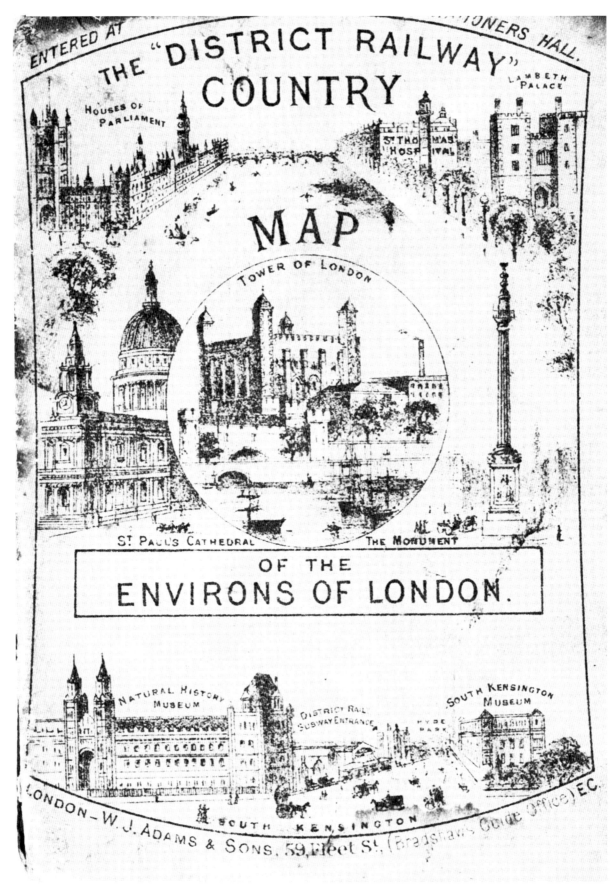

The District Railway was at first worked by the Metropolitan with four directors on the board with Sir John Fowler acting as Chief Engineer. This brought some dissatisfaction and they gave notice to the Met of eighteen months on January 3, 1870. It then ordered its own locomotives and rolling stock and began operating as such on July 3, 1871. The intensity of the District Railway system was spread throughout the city in a way that the Metropolitan was not.

Author's Collection

on the opening day which must have left the promoters flushed with excitement, it was after all only three miles 60 chains! Only a service interval of 15 minutes could have completed such intensity and attain such numbers, which says a great deal of the operating organisation allowing for regular watering of the engines in use. An alcove at Paddington station remains in possible mystification for modern travellers which was in fact the siding where they held the locomotives that would run out and back onto the trains for the return journey to Farringdon Street. Average daily passenger figures amounted to 2,500. Fares were single 6d (2½p) first class; 4d (1½p) second class; 3d (1p) third class. Return tickets 9d, 6d and 5d respectively. Annual season tickets £8 first; £5 ten shillings 2nd. Early morning workmen's tickets were 3d return.

There were five intermediate stations, Edgware Road, Baker Street, Portland Road, Gower Street and Kings Cross. Portland Street became Great Portland Street on March 1, 1917. Gower Street became Euston Square on November 1, 1909.

A suspension of activity occurred on Sunday mornings during the period of church services a practice that survived on the Met until October 1909.

All trains accommodated 1st, 2nd and 3rd classes until December 17, 1906 when classes were abolished. One wonders to what extent the class lines were diminished by the complexity of travelling en masse in such close confinement. The present use of the underground is, to say the least, endured in close proximity with ones fellow traveller. Imagine a period when women wore voluminous clothing indoors, and outdoors they added to it with yards of heavy cloth, wearing broad brimmed hats that had the look of inverted meat plates. These were never removed in public. Given the fact also that people bathed very little and effective deodorants were none existent. The introduction of escalators in 1911 would have proved perilous for women so there are good practical reasons for the rise of hemlines apart from the delight of the male population.

Early locomotives were of the broad gauge which put the matter firmly in the GWR camp although the line had been built in the mixed gauge, fortunately for the Metropolitan as it proved. The 22 coke burning 2-4-0 engines used were designed by Gooch. The first six were built by Vulcan Foundry and named 'Bee', 'Mosquito', 'Gnat', 'Hornet', 'Locust' and 'Wasp', an eccentric choice given that these applied to insects noted for their irritation to man with the exception of the 'Bee'.

The following six built by Kitson paid regard to the assertion of leadership by being called 'Czar', 'Kaiser', 'Khan', 'Shah', 'Mogul' and 'Bey'.

A further ten were built at Swindon in tribute to floral names. They all carried the innovation of outside cylinders in their design. The engineer for the line John Fowler tried to overcome the excessive smoke problems by designing a 'hot brick' locomotive which was not a success. It carried the slightly mocking name of 'Fowler's Ghost'.

Coach stock was supplied by the GWR which were 45 eight wheel compartment carriages of 42ft over the buffers. The four axles were grouped in pairs at each end but not bogies.

Six were old stock, plus six first and nine composite (first and second), 10 (second) and 14 (third class). The additionals were all newly built by Brown & Marshall of Birmingham.

The second and third class compartments carried six on each side. The roofs of the coaches carried the bags for coal gas lighting which gives a pale yellow blanching effect to people's faces. This being underground, it was something of an innovation over oil lighting.

Rails were of iron with steel surfaces to a depth of 1/16 inch flanged, weighing 62lb per yard and of the Vignoles pattern. It was no surprise given the intensive service that the surface perished rapidly and became liable to fracture. In 1866 the whole line was relaid with Bessemer steel rails in Vignoles pattern but at 86lb per yard, this was something more robust altogether with cross sleepers. The flange of the rail 6⅜ wide giving a greater bearing surface. Some points systems were built with manganese steel.

Signalling was of the mechanical as the Metropolitan was the first railway to be worked throughout on the absolute 'block' system with points and signals interlocked.

As the greater influence was from the GWR the Spagnoletti telegraph was used.

All of these features were adopted also by the erstwhile Metropolitan & District Railway that began to operate the southern part of the incomplete inner circle in 1868.

All did not remain as sweetness and companionship between the Met and GWR.

The extension of the line to Moorgate in 1865 was an advantage that the Metropolitan wished to retain to itself, restricting the interest of the GWR from increasing its original investment.

Thus a row took place between them that the Met must have been prepared for as the GWR took the ultimate sanction and threatened on July 18, 1863 that it would cease to work the railway from September 30. Rather coolly the Met replied that it would take over the system on October 1.

This must have incensed the GWR who then said that it would withdraw its rolling stock on August 10.

This was a bit of brinkmanship on the part of Myles Fenton, General Manager of the Met. In his application to the LNWR and GNR for assistance he must have had some confidence in the request for carriages. The early railway companies seemed to love out doing each other and quite a few rows had already taken place between the LNWR and GWR.

Steam locomotives were a problem as they had to be fitted able to work underground without emitting the steam and smoke normal on the surface.

The man of the hour was Archibald Sturrock, the Locomotive Superintendent of the GNR who had prepared some smoke-condensing loco-motives for the suburban service that the GNR were in anticipation of introducing from Kings Cross to Farringdon Street on September 1. The upshot was that Sturrock ingeniously fitted out some existing locos with a flexible pipe from the engine to the tender.

Thus standard gauge trains began working on August 11 and the GNR were able to introduce their suburban and City service on October 1.

In consequence the GWR withdrew from the undertaking as the Metropolitan began to run standard gauge stock. Nevertheless the GWR retained their investment interest in the underground railway particularly to Smithfield market.

The differences between the Met and GWR did mellow somewhat as the GWR began to run broad gauge trains through between Windsor and Farringdon Street and on the Hammer-smith branch and between Addison Road and the City.

The progress of the Metropolitan is truly remarkable when it is realised that the Hammersmith & City line was opened just over a year later after the first section on June 13, 1864.

An Act for the Notting Hill - Brompton extension from Paddington to South Kensington was accessioned on July 29. Whilst in the east an Act for the extension from Moorgate Street to Minories (Tower Hill Extension) was also in ascendancy. Moorgate station was opened on December 23 1865.

The Met built the Widened Lines which were opened on January 1, 1866.

The London, Chatham & Dover Railway made its approach from the south and built a connecting with the Met at Farringdon Street opened on January 1, 1866. After a bridge had been built across the Thames at Blackfriars over which the LCDR allowed the GNR to run over with a north south passenger service on February 20, 1866. This lasted until Jul 1, 1867 when all passenger services on the connections ceased. Thenceforth all LCDR trains reversed at Farringdon Street

The Smithfield Curve was put in to give connection for LCDR into Moorgate. It was only 16 chains long with 14 chains owned by Met and 2 chains owned by LCDR opened September 1, 1871. LCDR used the curve to Moorgate for the last time on April 1, 1916. It was not officially closed until 1927. Brick partitions were built and created rooms for a poultry store. In January 1958 a severe fire destroyed the Smithfield Poultry market and during the clearance of the ruined site the tunnel was re-discovered. The connection with the LCDR continued with freight trains of LNER and LMS going through the West Street Junction to run onto Southern lines.

The railway now begins to resemble a pair of calipers beckoning the closure of the gap. It was however to be a lessening of the pace with a separate railway being established that did not always see eye to eye with the extant Metropolitan. The south part of the Circle, became the domain of the Metropolitan &

continued on page 83

Advertisement of the stations on the District Railway's system it appears to make full use of the variety of printer's typefaces!

Author's Collection

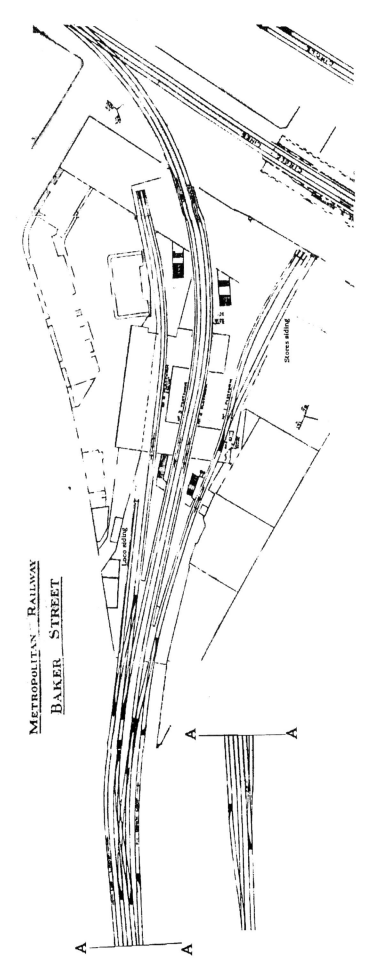

Plan view of the Baker Street junction station. This was originally the terminus of the St Johns Wood Railway that ran into the bay at the top of the plan. The siding at the bottom of the plan is where trains delivered coal to Chiltern Court.

Some important dates in the Development of the Underground Railways of London

Year	Railway	Date
1838	London & Greenwich (first line)	December 28
1853	Metropolitan Railway incorporated as North Metropolitan Railway	January
1854	Metropolitan Railway re-incorporated as a mixed gauge line from a junction with the Great Western Railway at Bishop's Road, Paddington to Victoria Street. (now Farringdon Street).	August 7
1863	Opening of first Underground (Metropolitan) line from Bishops Road to Farringdon Street..	January 10
1863	GWR give notice of termination of providing broad gauge locomotives and rolling to work the line at seven days notice.	August 10
1864	Opening of the Hammersmith & City Railway	June 13
1865	Farringdon Road - Moorgate extension	December 23
1866	Opening of Westbourne Park station	February 1
1866	Connection made with LCDR Blackfriars to Farringdon Street	January 1
1868	Opening of St John's Wood Railway to Swiss Cottage	April 13
1868	Opening of Latimer Road station	December 16
1868	Opening Praed Street - Bayswater - Notting Hill Gate - High Street (Kensington) - Gloucester Road.	October 1
1868	To South Kensington	December 24
1868	First section of District Railway opened from South Kensington to Westminster Bridge.	December 24
1868	Connection by Metropolitan with Midland Railway at Kings Cross.	
1868	District connect South Kensington to Westminster.	December 24
1869	Broad gauge rails removed from Metropolitan line.	
1869	District connect Gloucester Road with West Brompton	December 24
1870	District Westminster Bridge to Blackfriars	May 30

1870	District Gloucester Road to South Kensington	August 1
1870	District Cromwell Curve built without statutory authority	July 3
1871	District connect Blackfriars to Mansion House	July 3
1871	District connect Kensington High Street to Cromwell Road Junction	July 3
1871	District new lines through South Kensington Station	July 3
1872	District Earls Court Warwick Road Junction to West London Junction for Addison Road	February 1
1874	District Hammersmith extension: West Kensington East Junction to Hammersmith	September 9
1875	Connection made at Liverpool Street with GER	
1875	Opening Moorgate to Bishopsgate (Liverpool Street)	July 12
1876	Opening from Liverpool Street to Aldgate	November 18
1877	District reaches Hammersmith via LSWR. Hammersmith to Studland Road Junction	June 1
1879	Extension of St John's Railway from Swiss Cottage to West Hampstead	June
1879	District Ealing Extension Turnham Green to Ealing Broadway	July 1
1879	Extension of railway from West Hampstead to Willesden Green.	November 24
1880	Extension of railway from Willesden Green to Harrow	August 2
1880	District Fulham Ext West Brompton to Putney Bridge	March 1
1882	Aldgate to Tower Hill built and opened by Metropolitan Railway	September 25
1883	District connecting line with GWR at Ealing Broadway	March 1
1883	District Hounslow Extension Mill Hill Park to Hounslow Town	May 1
1884	District Hounslow Extension Osterley (Lampton Junction) to Hounslow Barracks	July 21
1884	Aldgate to Mansion House (Joint Met & Met & District)	October 6
1884	District Mansion House to Tower Hill	October 6
1884	Minories Junction to Whitechapel St Mary's Junction	October 6

1884	Whitechapel St Mary's Junction to Whitechapel	October 6
1885	Extension of railway from Harrow to Pinner	May 25
1887	Extension of railway from Pinner to Rickmansworth	September 1
1889	Putney Bridge to Wimbledon (LSWR)	June 3
1889	Extension of railway from Rickmansworth to Chesham	July 8
1890	Opening of the City & South London Railway (Tube)	December 18
1900	Extension to Moorgate Street	February 26
1900	Extension to Clapham Common	June 4
1901	Extension to Angel at Islington	November 17
1907	Extension to Euston	May 12
1891	Aylesbury & Buckingham Railway amalgamated with Metropolitan Railway. (Aylesbury to Verney Junction)	July 1
1891	Central London Railway incorporated by Act of Parliament	August 5
1892	Extension of railway from Rickmansworth to Aylesbury	September 1
1892	Great Northern & City Railway Act Finsbury Park to Moorgate Street	
1898	Waterloo & City Waterloo -Bank (The Drain) Began with using motorised coaches. Became part of Northern Line and British Rail ownership in 1994, now Network Rail	August 8
1899	Acton Town to South Acton (opened for goods) South Acton Station and line opened for passengers June 13, 1905	May 15
1900	Central London Railway between Bank and Shepherds Bush opened by Prince of Wales Passenger traffic	June 27 August
1902	Whitechapel & Bow Railway, Whitehapel to Campbell Road Junction, Bow with LTSR	June 2
1903	Ealing (Hanger Lane Junction) to Park Royal	June 23
1903	Park Royal to South Harrow	June 28
1904	Opening of Great Northern & City line to Moorgate	February 13
1904	Opening of Harrow to Uxbridge (worked by Metropolitan Railway, which acquired it from July 1 1905: District trains from March 1 1910	July 4

1904	Great Northern & City Railway opened Finsbury Park - Moorgate Now part of Network Rail built with main line loading gauge Bought by Metropolitan in 1913. In 1933 became Northern City line Last LT train ran October 4, 1975	February 14
1905	Act of Parliament passed for line between Harrow and Verney Junction be leased to the Metropolitan & Great Central Joint Committee.	
1905	Hounslow Town curve (abandoned May 1 1909	June 13
1906	Act of 1905 enforced by Met & GCR Joint Committee (Harrow to Verney Junction).	
1906	Baker Street & Waterloo Railway	April 2
1907	Charing Cross, Euston & Hampstead Railway	
1908	Central London Railway extension to Wood Lane 'Twopenny Tube' loco hauled.	May 14
1912	Extension of Central London Rly to Liverpool Street	
1912	Powers obtained by Metropolitan to extend Met & GCR Joint line from Rickmansworth to Croxley Green and Watford. Also for the widening of lines between Finchley Road and Wembley Park.	
1913	Metropolitan Railway take over the Great Northern & City Railway.	June 30
1913	Paddington extension, City Line	November
1914	Edgware Road extension	
1914	Embankment Extension, Charing Cross	April 6
1915	Queens Park - Willesden Junction Extension	May 10
1917	Watford Junction Extension 'Bakerloo'	April 16
1920	Extension of Central London Railway to Ealing Broadway acting on powers from 1911 to join with Ealing & Shepherds Bush Railway (GWR).	August
1923-4	Hendon & Edgware Extension of CCE&HR	November 19
1926	Kennington Extension	September 13

District Railway and by the completion did not connect finally until 1884. By now matters were in hand between Sir Edward Watkin, Chairman of the Metropolitan Railway and John Staats Forbes, Chairman of the Metropolitan & District Railway; to say they didn't get on would put it very lightly. This contributed to the strife of completing the inner Circle.

Electric power generation began in the 1870s and 1880s with small plants supplying localised use. This was of course the ideal power source to expand the railways of London's underground. Electrification came on the Underground with the first tube line The City & South London Railway in 1890. The Circle not until 1905 when Neasden power station came into use. From then on to Uxbridge making Harrow the change over point. In 1910 between Rayners Lane and South Harrow. On January 5, 1925 extended to Rickmansworth, also with the LNER from Moor Park to Watford. In 1960 work began on the £9,000,000 scheme to electrify the line from Rickmansworth to Amersham to be completed in September 11, 1961. This involved four tracking from Harrow on the Hill to Watford south junction. Also the widening of 13 bridges. The Ray Street Gridiron required extensive reinforcing in 1960 with a concrete raft 108ft in length to provide a new bridge deck. Also operating as a support between retaining walls. On completion the original girders were removed. The Met began to run trains to New Cross, South Eastern Railway on October 1, 1884. It was originally worked using the train staff and ticket method.

Interestingly even in the ascendant travails of war the Metropolitan Railway added a 1st class coach to the Great Northern & City section between Moorgate and Finsbury Park. This was the first occasion when a 'Tube' line received 1st class accommodation. Commencing on February 1st, 1915, for what was but a nine minute service.

Hammersmith & City

As the Circle struggled to be completed, a railway was promoted to Hammersmith in the west. This used the GWR between Bishop's Road and Westbourne Park and was promoted by the Hammersmith & City Railway incorporated on July 22, 1861, to build a branch of some 2¼ miles in mixed gauge from Green Lane Junction, later Westbourne Park, to a terminus near Hammersmith Broadway. It was opened on June 13, 1864 and worked by GWR until April 1, 1865.

The railway included a branch from Latimer Road to Uxbridge Road. Unlike the need to be underground by the Circle line the H&CR was able to elevate above the streets with stations also raised.

Broad gauge was removed between Hammersmith and Latimer Road in August 1868. Between Uxbridge Road and Westbourne Park on March 15, 1869.

By this time the GWR were building branches in standard gauge - Princes Risborough to Aylesbury being the first example. The Met absorbed H&MC in 1867.

Description of Journey in early days

Although the new railway had popular usage it must have been unnerving traveling through darkness with the unstable forces of fire, high pressure steam and water all moving at speed and confined with strangers. Even today in the age of electricity bright lighting and good draughting many people are still nervous of the underground.

A number of articles published under the title of 'Romance of Modern London' was published in the *English Illustrated Magazine* in 1894. One of them was of a footplate ride on the underground steam railway. It seemed to confirm all that could be imagined of this unnerving experience. Gothic black darkness with sudden sharp bright illumination showing, other persons and objects nearby that disappeared again with a return to the blackness pierced by vivid red and orange swirling sulphurous steam.

'Off again, a fierce light now trailing out behind us from the open furnace door, lighting up the fireman as he shovelled more coal on to the furnace, throwing great shadows into the air, and revealing overhead a low creamy roof with black lines upon it that seemed to chase and follow us. Ever and anon the Guard's face could be dimly seen at his window (a ducket window whereby the Guard could look along the train), more like a ghost than a man; while in the glass of the look-out holes reflected the forms of engine-men, like spirits of the tunnel mocking us from the black pit into which we were plunging.'

Smithfield Market

Peter Bush

An account of taking trains into Smithfield by Peter Bush, as a young fireman at Old Oak Common an engineman of the 1950s.

'One of the many turns that we had was collection a consignment of refrigerated wagons from Acton goods yard for delivery to the rail terminal at Smithfield Market in London.

On departing from the yard with 12 wagons full of meat with a GWR 0-6-0 tank engine. We were routed main line to Paddington goods where we would join the London underground system.

Our engine was fitted with a steam condenser that diverts all the exhaust steam into the engine's water tanks. The system was operated by a lever in the cab and was only used when the engine was required to operate on London underground as they did not want steam in the tunnels.

One of the drawbacks of using the condenser was the lack of blast from the exhaust pipes to draw the fire. Like all steam engines the greater the blast the more efficient the engine would perform. With all the steam going into the water tanks there was no blast to draw the fire. The only blast would be the use of the engine's blower this is operated manually from the cab.

When this method was operated it creates a problem for the fireman, with no blast to the fire he must go into the tunnels with a lot of fire and no unburnt coal.

Whilst driving on the underground system one of the safety features they had was at every signal there was a small protruding bar that was up when the signal was red, on the engine we had a bar facing down, if the engine passed the signal on red both bars would touch moving the engine bar up which would bring the train to a halt.

If stopped the fireman would have to get down from the engine and reset the bar.

Our train would now proceed onto the underground towards Farringdon street where, just beyond we would branch off to the left into a small goods yard at Smithfield Market.

On arriving the shunter would unhook the engine and call us forward to a small engine parking bay. There were about six bays for unloading the trucks. The shunter would unhook each wagon then attach a rope around the draw hook the other end was attached to a capstan, which revolved on a vertical axis drawing the wagon. The capstan was operated by the shunter via a small button on the floor.

Using this method all wagons were despatch into their separate bays.

By necessity diagrammatic drawings show the lines of the underground yard in nice straight lines. My experience was that they were worn and twisted moving the engine around all the time.

On departing with empty wagons we went straight back to Acton Goods Yard.

If we managed to get out straight away we continued the shift doing shunting at Acton and sometimes take empty coach stock into Paddington station. The big fear was to get out as quickly as you could before the rush hour traffic started; because if you get delayed by longer period of shunting and were still down there at 7.30 you had to stay there until 11 o' clock and believe me it was no place to want to stay.'

Roy Miller

One of the founder members of the Quainton Railway Society in 1964. He has served a long period of dedicated service in many offices of the Society that could not have prospered without his contribution. He has contributed the following to this history describing the underground area below Smithfield Market in the midst of the bombing during Word War II.

'My Father used to buy meat for the remaining family luncheon restaurants in the city of London. Sometimes if he needed to visit Smithfield Market on a Saturday he would take me with him, at this time we were living with Gran in Little Chalfont as our house in Dollis Hill had been bombed.

We had not been in the office of the person my Father had come to see very long before the Air Raid Siren sounded. My Father's friend said

The junction at the east end of Farringdon Street station of the lines to Moorgate on the left and the line of the original London, Chatham & Dover Railway on the right going south over the river

Bill Simpson

"follow me" and we walked a short distance through the market to a large black and white sign saying 'Shelter' where we were joined by another group of people going down a flight of wrought iron stairs, imagine my joy to find we were in a railway goods yard. There were quite number of box vans some of the special insulated type and others normal box vans, this was obviously where the GWR pannier tanks came after they had thundered through Baker Street on the Inner Circle. There were no locomotives and the box vans were empty but strong smell of recently unloaded meat lingered with the familiar smell of a lingering steam as in a locomotive yard.

We walked along a platform between the box vans, down some steps and into another tunnel which had no railway in it but was obviously a disused railway tunnel. The tunnel had a large arched roof or at least seemed to have to a small boy, there were many chairs and a few beds behind screens obviously to stop the draft, also a refreshment counter which was closed much to my Father's disappointment. The main purpose of the shelter was for night time use and could easily have held several hundred people.

Quite soon the "all clear" sounded, we said good-bye to my Father's friend and continued to walk further along the tunnel to where there was a temporary staircase, an Ar Raid Warden or someone in uniform opened a door for us and we were out in a street some way from the market. I cannot remember quite where it was, I have always thought it was part of the then disused Thames Link tunnels but it may also have been the abandoned spur into the Smithfield Market from the LSWR not shown on many maps. It was quite near Holborn Viaduct in Farringdon Street as we continued our walk to see the site of one of my Father's restaurants which had been bombed a few weeks previously, about a hundred yards or so from the Viaduct.

Being a Saturday my Father had to report for Civil Defence duty in Willesden overnight as he did for most of the war, he put me on the train at Baker Street in the front compartment so I could get a better view of the locomotive change at Rickmansworth where the steam locomotive came on and waved good-bye. I felt very grown up and so ended another day I shall never forget.'

Early photograph of A class no 6 at Finchley Road. It was given the name 'Medusa' and was withdrawn in 1906.
K A C R Nunn

An early photograph of one of the Metropolitan & District Railway tank engines virtually in original form.

An Ealing bound train on the District Railway line from Gloucester Road hauled by A class no 34.

MDR 4-4-0 tank no 33 built 1880 it was scrapped in 1925.

An A class no 20 possibly at Hammersmith on September 9, 1898. The livery would suggest the early period which for a time was green. The engine eventually went to the Nidd Valley Light Railway.

R K Blencowe

An A class No 26 in original cabless condition. The man in the foreground is holding a shunter's pole, used to hook and unhook wagons.

Great Western & Metropolitan Joint Stock train motor unit no 2243 at Farringdon Street on July 10, 1937. These units were introduced in 1906 for working the Hammersmith & City service.

Barry Tucker Collection

Moorgate station on June 23, 1961.

H C Casserley

One of the MetroVick locos on the siding at Baker Street. This engine no 4 'Lord Byron' apparently to work a train to Neasden.

The E class at Edgeware Road in on the SLS Railtour.

H C Casserley

A photograph taken during the building of the Barbican complex above Moorgate in the 1960s. The train is one of the sub surface O and P stock units fitted with Metadyne traction motors. An example train is held at the Buckinghamshire Railway Centre at Quainton Road station.

T J Edgington

A special run for the Stephenson Locomotive Society on Sunday, September 22, 1957 using E class L46. This was on Hammersmith & City and Circle lines. From Edgware Road at 2.32 pm to Hammersmith hauled by electric locomotive. Upon return to Edgeware Road hauled by L46 to South Kensington, Mansion House and Liverpool Street. Then non stop to Wembley Park where the tour ended at 5.07 pm.

In celebratory style L44 (Met 1) was able to return in January 2013 and run between Kensington Olympia and Moorgate again for the 150 Anniversary of the worlds first underground railway.

H C Casserley

The railway beneath the streets reassured with exquisite gleaming tiles and artfully conceived colour schemes as at the Baker Street Booking Hall.

Tfl From the London Transport Museum Collection

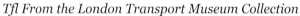

For the first time in the world, the proposed Baker Street passenger station, on a railway beneath the ground. Note the lines of mixed gauge. At the beginning of the twentieth century the elegant Chiltern Court would rise above this, covering the lunettes from appreciative sunlight.

TfL from the London Transport Museum Collection

Baker Street exterior 1885-1895. Imagine, the clatter of hundreds of horse hooves and rumble of wheels, softer with the Hansoms but louder with steel rimmed horse omnibuses and carriers carts. Whilst those that needed had to shout above the din!

TfL from the London Transport Museum Collection

Bowler hatted gents go about their business passing beautifully lined out and lettered T stock car no 2751 at Baker Street.

TfL from the London Transport Museum Collection

The frontage of Kew Gardens station the light coloured brickwork and 'Italian' influence of the round topped windows presents a pleasing design to complement a leafy suburb environment.

Bill Simpson

The District line station of Kew Gardens on the line to Upminster.

Bill Simpson

The Manning Wardle engine 'Huddersfield' at the Brill line platform at Quainton Road with the typical train assembly during Oxford & Aylesbury Tramway days. The old Wotton Tramway coach by the Ashbury Carriage Co. is near the engine. Behind this is one of the bogie vehicles of the Bristol Carriage & Wagon Co which was accessed on the open verandahs at each end. Unseen behind this would be a three plank wagon with milk churns.

Locomotive Publishing no 3282

Locomotives and Passenger Stock

The Met had some 0-6-0 tanks built by Worcester Engine Co in 1868 for the St John's Wood Railway, they left after a few years service, too powerful. Which rather suggests probably heavy on coal.

The steam locomotives were split into seven types prefixed with a letters A, C, D, F G, H, K. In 1897 and 1899 two Peckett & Co 0-6-0 saddle tanks were put into service that were not classified as such. These were used for shunting at Neasden and Harrow.

Met engines at the outset had been painted green but with the development of the Metropolitan & District locos in green the Met changed to a deep rich red colour. They also carried their numbers in brass on the front of the chimney but with the change of livery this was discontinued.

A class

A batch of locomotives were ordered by Joseph Tomlinson, Locomotive Superintendent of the Metropolitan Railway these were built in 1879-

80 by Beyer Peacock & Co Ltd. The earliest purchase was by Sir John Fowler they entered service in October, 1864 and numbered 1 to 18 and 19 to 23 they were delivered in 1866. Further nos 25 to 28 came in 1868 whilst Nos 29 to 39 were delivered in 1869 followed by nos 40 to 44 in 1870.

Locomotive needs must have been pressing with the success of the Underground where these locomotives had proved worthy to the task more were needed. Consequently came additions 45 to 59 with increased boiler pressure and tank and bunker capacity. Further additions came in 1884 with nos 60 to 64.

Upon his occupation of the post of Locomotive Superintendent in 1885 Mr J J Hanbury added more with nos 65 and 66.

Interestingly similar locos were built for the District Railway which rather proves the satisfaction of their use, also the Midland Railway.

The derivation of this flexible wheelbase design is seen in a 4-4-0 tank engine designed by Mr John Chester Craven whilst Locomotive Superintendent of the London, Brighton & South Coast Railway and built in 1859. It shows remarkable early development of the form with a leading bogie, four coupled wheels and outside cylinders.

The A class no 23 built in 1866 went to Clapham Railway Museum on January 15, 1961. Restored to its 1903 condition. It was painted in Crimson Lake livery with yellow lining. The cab was removed and the chimney altered. It had been rebuilt three times, 1889, 1903 and 1918. It worked on the Inner Circle until 1905 following electrification. From 1905 until 1914 it headed trains between Baker Street and Rickmansworth, Chesham and Verney Junction. It then worked on shunting at Neasden yard with occasional trip coal workings. From there it was sent to work on the Brill branch. After the closure of the branch in 1935 it went shunting again at Neasden and Lillie Bridge. Its outstanding train working was in 1934 when an eleven coach train from Leicester failed at Aylesbury and no 23 had to take it forward to Marylebone. What an expression there must have been on the faces of Brill line footplate men in their reserve of country branch line insouciance, drawing on a pipeful of baccy as they easily coasted along the branch suddenly being instructed to make haste to Aylesbury and attach to the waiting train for London!

C Class

The Four C class locos built by Nielson & Company in 1891 showed an influence of South Eastern Railway in design. Possibly the influence of Sir Edward Watkin as he was Chairman of that company also. They were entrusted with trains on the heavily graded section through the Chilterns to help out the A class. They were introduced in 1891 and the first was withdrawn in 1917 whilst all the others went in 1923.

D Class

In 1894 six Sharp Stewart 2-4-0 tanks know as D class were introduced these stubby little 2-4-0s were intended for the lines north of Aylesbury where they began service on February 1, 1895. They were not a great success in their role,

especially taking over on some duties on the Brill line which in its rustic form proved difficult, leaving the Manning Wardles to continue in splendid exclusion. Now painted red and lined in yellow with 'MR' on their buffer beam. Until the A class displaced them. The MW 'Brill No 1' was seen in 1924 working on the building of the Great West Road. As it was dealing with contractors wagon it had been fitted with dumb buffers. A roughly built engine shed was constructed whilst the engine was working on the temporary railway.

E class

In 1896 the Met brought in E class designed by Met Loco Superintendent T F Clark. The first three were built in the Met works at Neasden one being given the number 1 replacing an A class loco with that number.

Four more E class were built by Hawthorn, Leslie & Co Ltd in 1900-01.

This class was destined to endure with the no 1 passing into preservation to the Quainton Railway Society. It had enjoyed an illustrious past by hauling the first train to Uxbridge June 30, 1904. During its career Met 1 was chartered by the Southern Railways Touring Society for a Metropolitan Railtour on Sunday, October 1, 1961. A train of Aylesbury line compartment stock ran from Wembley Park to Stanmore, then to Baker Street along the Inner Circle to Liverpool Street. Then by Aldgate east and the rarely used St Mary's Curve to the East London line and through the Thames Tunnel to New Cross Gate. Here the electric locomotive 'Oliver Goldsmith' took over the train and returned to Baker Street

After many years serving at the Buckinghamshire Railway Centre the footlights called once more and it travelled back to its London origins and looking resplendent hauling an equally shining train from Kensington Olympia to Moorgate on January 13, 2013 to celebrate 150 years of the world's first Underground Railway.

F Class

In 1901 the F class locos appeared being for 0-6-2 tanks built by the Yorkshire Engine Company. These were intended for freight working. They had a similar look to the E class.

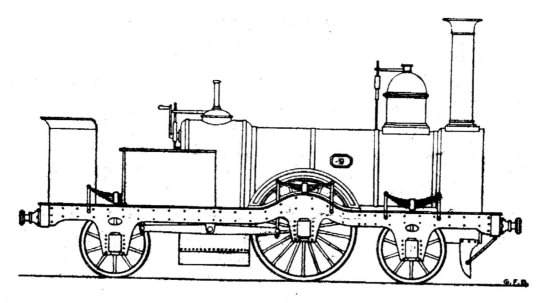

A number of engines were converted by GNR to work the Underground during the period of the GWR withdrawal. This is how the converted engine looked, it was something of a stop gap until new engines for the Met could be delivered.

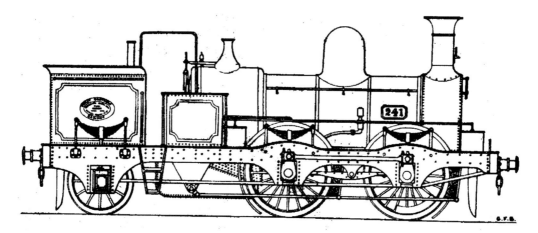

More purposeful designs were completed by Archibald Sturrock in 1865 and built by the Avonside Engine Co of Bristol. Condensing was done by means of a long pipe running below the footplate into the water tank. These sturdy engines hauled the early standard gauge trains for the Met.

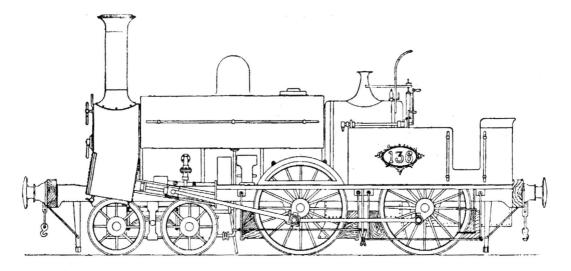

The development of the ubiquitous 'A' tank engines found their origins from a design by John Chester Craven on the LB&SCR. The wheel arrangement and the inclined cylinders are obvious indications of descent. Engine 136 ran from 1859 until 1874.

Engine no 23 at Neasden in 1937, her tenure on the Brill branch completed she returned to shunting duties at the yard.

Barry Tucker Collection

G Class

The next locos were the 0-6-4 G class from Yorkshire Engine Company in 1915. These were given names. 'Lord Aberconway', the last Chairman of the Metropolitan Railway, 'Robert H Selbie', General Manager of the Metropolitan Railway from 1908-1930, 'Charles Jones' the company's Chief Locomotive & Electrical Engineer. The engine 'Brill' seems oddly out of step with these luminaries, it was given this name as it was considered the furthest station on the Met. The most eccentric certainly, but geographically Verney Junction must have had that feature as it was 6 miles 36 chains from Quianton Road, whereas Brill was 6 miles 22 chains leaving a distinction of 14 chains.

H Class

In 1920-1 came the H class, eight in number, built by Kerr Stewart & Co designed by Charles Jones. These locos appear prominent in the closing years of steam on the Met as they were introduced in 1920. They had the distinction of being transferred to the LNER to continue service with that company from 1937 until complete withdrawal between 1942 and 1947. When LT took over the Met in 1933 the line still had 30 steam locomotives.

From 1925 only the lines north of Rickmansworth needed steam locos for passenger work.

K Class

The Metropolitan had operated from its beginnings with engines of no more than 0-6-4 wheel arrangement. In 1925 this was changed by the introduction of the 87 tons K class with a tractive effort of 24,400lb. Six of them built by Armstrong Whitworth for hauling heavy freight on the outer lines of the system. They used parts made at Woolwich Arsenal post WW1. The parts were of the SECR design.

The Met did have a considerable volume of freight traffic, unlike most of the other underground railways which was handled by these locos.

GWR Panniers

GWR panniers came to LPTB on trial in 1956. The first was 7711 followed with a further thirteen.

The popular Manning Wardle engines were not only in service on the Brill line but another 0-6-0 called 'Nellie' was used by the contractors building the Uxbridge Railway which it seems drifted into Metropolitan use for shunting duties at Neasden.

Electrification

Electric services on the Metropolitan began on January 1, 1905 with multiple unit trains. This was done in economic justification as far as Harrow. Steam continuing onwards north.

Two batches of 10 electric locomotives were built by the Metropolitan Carriage & Wagon Co Ltd. The first 10 1905-06 fitted with Westinghouse equipment, and in the second batch that came in 1907-08 they had British Thomson-Houston equipment. The two types differed radically in appearance, No 1 to 10 were 'camel-back' or steeple cab design with a central driving position. The following nos 11 to 20 were box like in shape.

With electrification, the first changing point for steam and electric was Willesden Green. From 1906 this became Wembley Park. The advance to Harrow came on July 19, 1908. Further progress had to wait until January 5, 1925 when the current reached Rickmansworth.

MetroVick 'Sarah Siddons' type

In 1922 and 1923 the appreciative profile of Metropolitan-Vickers Limited locomotives arrived, one of which is preserved in Covent Garden Museum LT Collection. These were introduced with nos 1 to 20 built in Barrow-in-Furness. It was these engines that performed with exceptional dexterity, in company with their steam partners, doing change over duets at Rickmansworth. Their original nameplates which they received in 1926 had a period influence with an art nouveau design in cast brass, these were removed in 1942-43. They received their names back again in 1953. The new nameplates were in aluminium alloy, less decorative in the sans serif style, but one much appreciated by London Transport. A wartime scrap requirement of the originals seems very desperate, to have such a need to melt down pieces of typographic art. Locomotive No 8 was the first to be painted in grey. After the second world war the wartime grey was replaced with lined maroon livery.

The locomotives were withdrawn in 1961 when no 18 'Michael Faraday' took out a grand tour of enthusiastic followers on September 9 from Baker Street to Rickmansworth. From there the train of seven compartment type coaches were handed over to 2-6-4 tank no 42070. In the same celebratory form 'Sarah Siddons' also joined the steam locomotive Met with the run on January 13, 2013

The locomotives were 39ft 6in long and had suspended on each of the two four-wheel bogies 300 hp motor. Collecting shoes for dc current were four, two on each shoe beam, two negative shoes fixed to brackets on each outer motor casing.

They weighed 61½ tons and had a tractive effort of 22,000lb. Accelerating from standing to 25 mph in as many seconds. This was bound to be an asset even though it does not sound spectacular on speeds of today. But 65 mph top speed was plenty for frequent stops and hauling a 265 ton freight train up a 1 in 45 gradient is no mean accomplishment. They could also shunt at 2 mph and with a short wheelbase that could negotiate 3 chain curves.

By 1953 only 17 were locos left. Nos 15, 17, 19 were damaged at various times.

No 9 taken was taken out of passengers service, its vacuum brake removed. No 20 was scrapped following an accident in 1954.

Carriage & Multiple Unit Stock

On the opening of the Underground Railway the stock was supplied by the GWR eight wheel stock 38 feet long known as 'Long Charlies'. Flexibility for tight curves was achieved by allowing the axleboxes to move laterally in the hornguides.

After the dispute between the GWR and Met vehicles were loaned from the GNR and LNWR.

These were replaced with 34 new coaches from the Ashbury Carriage & Iron Company in October 1863. Onwards to 1866 more coaches were ordered from the Oldbury Carriage Co totalling 92. In 1868 50 more from Ashbury brought this to 142.

Carriages produced from 1879-1884 were built by Ashbury, Brown Marshall and Cravens adding 121 vehicles.

Staff of Neasden pose for a photograph on no 23 with a good array of Stephenson, Clark wagons on the siding behind.

Barry Tucker Collection

Given the sharp curvature on the Underground the Met introduced sets of two four-wheel coaches built by the Railway Carriage Company in 1869.

The service to Pinner and Rickmansworth brought a need for more stock in 1887 with new four-wheel coaches. Three complete trains of 9 vehicles were built by Craven Brothers of Sheffield and were used later on trains to Aylesbury. These were named Jubilee stock to celebrate the occasion of Queen Victoria's Diamond Jubilee. They were finally withdrawn in 1912.

On chassis donated by the Quainton Railway Society London Transport Museum were able to have built a body replica of one of these coaches to be in trains celebrating 150 years of the Underground Railway in 2013.

The need for better coaches with higher speed riding ability came in the 1890s and by 1898 better riding bogie stock was being employed, supplied by Ashbury Carriage & Iron Company. In April 1899 one train was built at Neasden and also Ashbury a repeat of an earlier order costing. Also further work undertaken by Cravens for two sets. All of these orders were placed in service in 1900.

The service to Verney Junction also utilised the new stock with trains often running with a four-wheel luggage van or a four wheel coach. They continued running north steam hauled until being converted to electric traction between 1906 to 1924. Six were re-converted for steam haulage for use on the Chesham branch from which they were withdrawn on September 1960. One was preserved by the Museum of British Transport and four went to the Bluebell Railway. It appears that some of these were shipped to France during the WW1 and stayed their being used on French Railways.

A joint Metropolitan Railway and Metropolitan & District Railway electrification experimental train built in 1899 and was tested between Earls Court and High Street Kensington in 1900.

Pullmans 'Mayflower' and 'Galatea' were put into service on June 1, 1910 between Baker Street to Aylesbury and Chesham and Verney Junction making several journeys each day including evening trips. First used with Ashbury stock then later with Dreadnought coaches.The coaches remained the property of the Pullman Car Co which charged a supplementary fee of 6d per fare between London and Rickmansworth. For journeys north of Rickmansworth an extra shilling was charged. They were withdrawn at

One of the 0-4-4 C class engines on a Verney Junction train. Note the early system of raised numbers on the chimney. This engine was withdrawn in 1923.

the outbreak of World War One and returned after to run to Aylesbury only. They were withdrawn again on October 7, 1939 with the outbreak of World War Two. They did not return.

In July 1905 two sets of four coaches were equipped with through control lines, dual braking system with driving trailer equipment for propulsion by saloon style Westinghouse 600 hp motor cars on the extended lines to Harrow. North of Harrow to be hauled by steam locomotives. Also to supplement services on the Circle lines. The sets proved difficult to use on regular stops services so new control gear and 800 hp saloon motor cars of the British Thomson-Houston were substituted.

The Ashbury stock were replaced with the new coaches called Dreadnoughts. Two five coach trains were introduced 1909-1910. Four more trains in 1911-12. Produced by the Metropolitan Carriage & Wagon Finance Co. Two more batches arrived in 1919-20 and 1922-23 of 42 and 20 vehicles respectively. The early vehicles were gaslit but subsequent risk of fire brought about electric lighting on those that followed. These became the standard vehicles seen on trains going north on Metropolitan lines until the end of the company.

In 1927 fifteen vehicles were converted for use in electric multiple unit trains. Five coaches being marshalled between new driving motor coaches to make three of the first trains of what is now known as the T stock. Ten further coaches were later similarly converted at various dates

Neasden shed on September 6, 1937 with one of the 0-6-2 goods engines no 92 of the F class. Cylinders 17¼ x 26; Pressure 160lbs; wheels 5ft; surface 1,150sq ft; weight 56 tons.

Barry Tucker Collection

Neasden 6/9/37 with one of the 0-6-2 goods tank locomotives no 92 built by the Yorkshire Engine Co in 1901. Cyls 17¼x 26; Pressure 160 lbs; driving wheels 5 ft; surface 1,150 sq. ft; weight 56 tons.

Barry Tucker Collection

by LT. Eventually T stock consisted of 60 driving motor coaches and 97 trailer coaches. That energetic decade of unrestrained hubris the 1960s saw their replacement with A stock of unpainted aluminium with the by now familiar sliding doors system of moving passengers.

Amersham, Chesham, Watford saw 8-coach A60 stock arrive on June 12 1961.

Final running of Metropolitan electric locomotives and steam stock was on September 9, 1961.

One of the fleet of exGWR panniers no L 90 that were utilised on various duties when electricity was switched out, particularly engineers' trains.

H C Casserley

From the origins of the 'Tube' the resolute little electric locomotive first used on the City & South London Railway stands in the isolated space of a bomb damaged Moorgate.

H C Casserley

One of the 0-4-4 passenger stock locomotive no 77. This locomotive together with nos 1 to 78 were built in the Company's works at Neasden in 1896. Cylinders 17¼ x 26; Pressure 160 lbs; wheels 5' 6"; surface 1,146 sq. ft; weight 54 tons.

Barry Tucker Collection

The E class in its new role with London Transport looking particularly brilliant in the shed at Neasden.
H C Casserley

Metropolitan Railway Railway 0-4-4 tank no 1 at Neasden coal pits. This locomotive hauled the special trains for the opening of the Harrow - Uxbridge Railway on June 30, 1904. It was fully decorated with the colours of the parent company, even the coal was painted white!

Barry Tucker Collection

One of the F class now L50 from its original Met no 91 at Neasden. It was withdrawn in 1958.

Barry Tucker Collection

Metropolitan Railway Neasden 0-6-4 passenger tank loco G class No. 94 'Lord Aberconway'. Built by the Yorkshire Engine Co Ltd in 1915.

Barry Tucker Collection

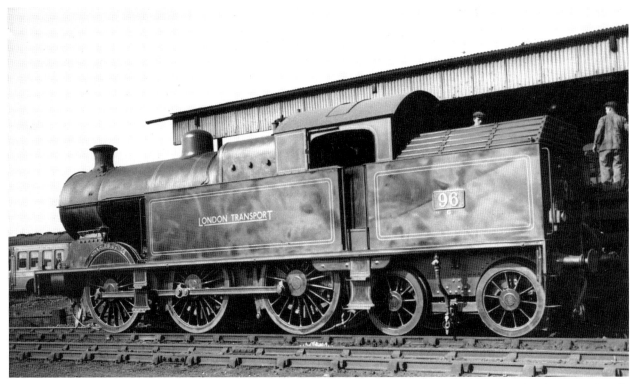

At the Neasden coaling stage one of the G class 0-6-4 passenger tank locomotives no 96 'Charles Jones' Built by Yorkshire Engine Co Ltd in 1915. Cyls 20 x 26; Pressure 60 lbs; Wheels 5' 9"; Surface 1,361 sq ft; weight 93 tons.

Barry Tucker Collection

Met Rly Neasden 4-4-4 tank diagrammed for working passenger stock. Locomotive no 103 is with its driver Charles Simmonds seen standing on the frame.

Barry Tucker Collection

One of the H class locomotive serving as 6420 under the LNER ownership in unlined black.

H C Casserley

As London Transport in September 1937 at Neasden a 2-6-4 goods loco no 115 built by Woolwich Arsenal in 1925. Cyls 19 x 28; Pressure 200lbs; wheels 5' 6"; surface 1,811 sq. ft; weight 87 tons 7 cwt.

Barry Tucker Collection

A K class no 111 obviously occupied, in steam at Neasden in 1937.

Barry Tucker Collection

Neasden 0-6-0 shunting saddle tank loco no 101 built by Peckett & Sons of Bristol in 1899. Cyls 16 x 22; Pressure 140 lbs; surface 712 sq. ft; wheels 3' 10"; weight 39 tons.

Barry Tucker Collection

A view of the other Peckett no 101 withdrawn 1960.

H C Casserley

Early electric loco No. 1 a train of non bogie carriages at Neasden circa 1905.
TfL from the London Transport Museum Collection

London Transport train the 12.41 pm to Chesham leaving Wembley Park behind former Metropolitan Electric locomotive No 15 'Wembley Exhibition 1924' with standard steam stock.

Barry Tucker Collection

Met Rly Electric locomotives at Neasden sheds led by no 5 'John Hampden'.

G B Penny

Old and the new at Wembley Park station. Modern elliptical roof stock alongside 1905 clerestory stock, July 7, 1937.

G B Penny

Electric train sets, 1905 clerestory stock train. On left an elliptical roofed train motor coach vehicle converted from coach.
Barry Tucker Collection

One of the early British Thomson Houston locomotives that were used before the now familiar MetroVick engines.

London Transport Society

Great Western & Metropolitan Joint Stock train. Motor unit no 2243 (introduced in 1906) at Farringdon Street July 10, 1937.

Barry Tucker Collection

Neasden with 1905 clerestory roofed third class corridor coach in Metropolitan livery. BTH/West 48 seats No. 9586 ex motor car no 29.

Barry Tucker Collection

Met Rly Train of old steam passenger stock (1870-1911) at Neasden yard.

Barry Tucker Collection

Metropolitan Railway luggage/passenger brake van no 6 at Neasden yard.
Barry Tucker Collection

Metropolitan Railway horse boxes no 5 Amersham and no 7 Harrow at Neasden.
Barry Tucker Collection

Met Rly Metropolitan Multiple units electric trains to Baker Street approaching Wembley Park.
Barry Tucker Collection

Motor unit coach no 2551 of elliptical roof stock (circa 1913) at Neasden bound for Aldgate July 15, 1937.
Barry Tucker Collection

Third class passenger coach with brake compartment no 8 1871-1905. This coach had a strip of carpet along the wooden seats and oil gas lighting (not incandescent).

Pullman car 'Galatea' in dark red livery on the City - Aylesbury service in the 1930s.

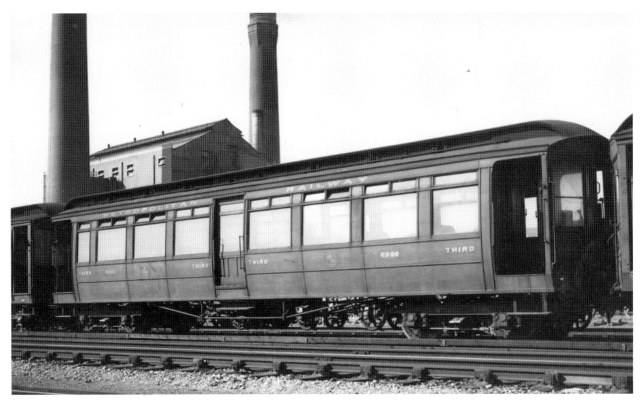

Met Rly Neasden Ex Great Northern & City coach (1902) in Metropolitan livery These coaches, although of timber type construction, are larger than those of the London Electric Railway, as when the line was constructed there was a proposition to run the GNR trains over the system in order to give them direct access to the City (Moorgate station via Finsbury Park) This scheme never materialised. The Great Northern & City Railway was absorbed by the Metropolitan Company in 1912.

Barry Tucker Collection

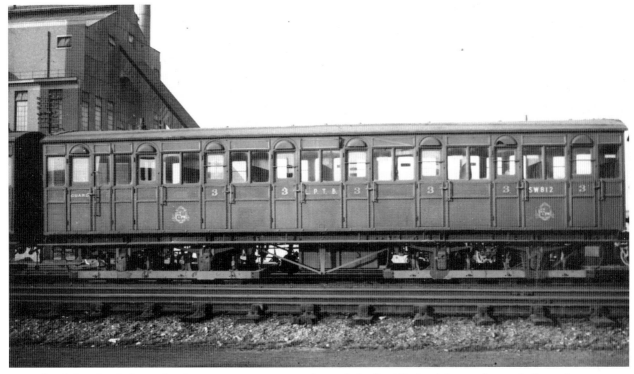

Met Rly Eight wheeled, non bogie passenger steam stock coach, built 1882(weight 24 1/2 tons). Ceased passenger work on the Brill branch in 1930 approx. Seen here in use as a frost scraper. See frames built round the wheels sets showing the brushes.

Barry Tucker Collection

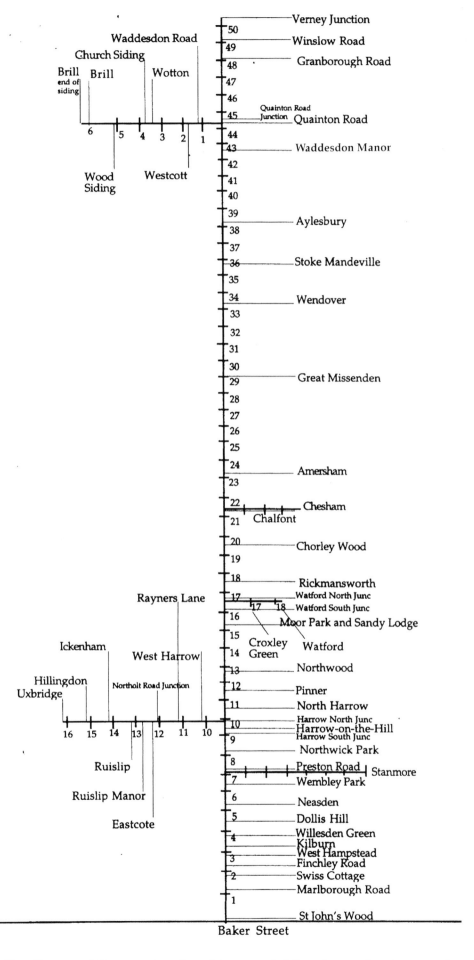

A line diagram of distances in miles of the extended lines from Baker Street station.

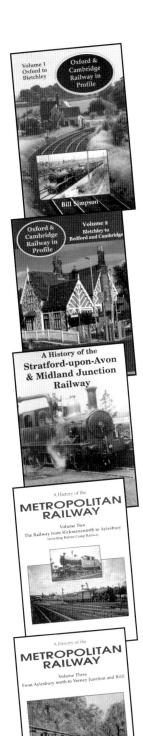

Other publications from Lamplight

Oxford to Cambridge Railway in Profile vol 1 (Oxford to Bletchley)
ISBN: 978 1 899246 16 8

This cross-country line of over thirty miles has had a remarkable past as the part of the 'Varsity' route. Operated by the LNWR until 1923 from the unusual station building at Oxford, now removed to the Buckinghamshire Railway Centre. The line called at the market towns of Bicester, and Winslow with several smaller stations between. The ninety-six pages contain 150 photographs, maps and diagrams. It is a line that would not fade away and is now likely to spring to a very active life once more as part of the new East West Railway promised in 2017.

Oxford to Cambridge Railway in Profile vol 2 (Bletchley to Cambridge)
ISBN: 978 1 899246 25 0

The second part of this history review centres on the successful survival of the line between Bletchley and Bedford that retained its full passenger service and has recently been upgraded. The story continues with illustrations and text on the section that was lost entirely between Bedford and Cambridge with many photographs not seen before. It is a story to enlighten as the prospect of a new Cambridge connection may soon to be realised. A through route that was lost now showing great promise.

Stratford-upon-Avon & Midland Junction Railway
ISBN: 978 1 899246 20 5

Fascinatingly detailed account of this remarkable railway that ran across the south midlands connecting with the LNWR/LMS, GWR, GCR and Midland Railway. The 160 page contain well over two hundred photographs, maps and diagrams with a very informative text. An essential definitive history of this line.

A History of the Metropolitan Railway vol 2
ISBN: 978 1 899246 08 3

Recent celebrations of the London Underground 150 particularly refer to the Metropolitan Railway as the first company to start the development of the system. In 160 pages the line is followed from Rickmansworth to Aylesbury, including the Halton Camp Railway. Highly visual with over two hundred photographs, maps and diagrams covering the subject including the Chesham branch.

A History of the Metropolitan Railway vol 3
ISBN: 978 1 899246 13 7

The Vale of Aylesbury has fascinated railway enthusiasts for many years in its remarkable diversity. The Metropolitan Railway, the Great Central Railway, the Great Western Railway and London & North Western Railway all ran through it. Eccentrically also the short six mile branch to Brill from Quainton Road Station. This history covers the subject in detail with so many fine photographs and line diagrams that could be used to explore the history of these lines in very pleasant countryside.

A History of the Railways of Oxfordshire: Part 1 The North
ISBN: 978 1 899246 02 1

A two volume history of Oxfordshire Railways complete with 250 photographs, maps, diagrams and a text that includes accounts from people that did the jobs needed to keep the railway running. It includes also a section on the Oxfordshire Ironstone Railway and the Bicester Military Railway. Casebound in 192 pages.

A History of the Railways of Oxfordshire: Part 2 The South
ISBN: 978 1 899246 06 9

With over two hundred photographs, maps and diagrams this book covers south Oxfordshire Railways including the line from Princes Risborough through Thame, to Oxford. Also the Abingdon and Watlington branches plus the Wantage Tramway. Casebound of 192 pages.

A History of the Bedford and Hitchin Railway
(Forthcoming)
The popularity of this publication has not only warranted a reprint but also an expanded story with further illustrations. Check for availability - it may be available when you read this.